Chapter 11

Business Reorganizations

For
Business Leaders,
Accountants
and Lawyers

Myles H. Alderman, Jr., Esq.

Outskirts Press, Inc.
Denver, Colorado

Chapter 11
Business Reorganizations
For Business Leaders, Accountants and Lawyers
All Rights Reserved
Copyright © 2006 Myles H. Alderman, Jr.

No copyright claimed for official government statutes or rules

"Practical & Tactical"™ is a trademark of Myles H. Alderman, Jr.

Outskirts Press
http://www.outskirtspress.com

ISBN-10: 1-59800-413-1
ISBN-13: 978-1-59800-413-7

Printed in the United States of America

About the Author

Attorney Myles Alderman has been representing debtors, creditors, creditors committees and other parties in interest in Chapter 11 Business Reorganizations and alternative business solutions since 1986. His clients include professional services firms, manufacturers, distributors, retailers and financial institutions ranging in size from closely held businesses to some the largest corporations in the world.

Mr. Alderman is a member of the Business Bankruptcy Section of the American Bar Association, The Business Bankruptcy Section of the American Bankruptcy Institute, and The Executive Committee of the Commercial Law and Bankruptcy Section of the Connecticut Bar Association. He was educated at Kenyon College (A.B. Economics & Psychology), Cambridge University (Post-Grad. Economics), and Syracuse University College of Law (J.D. Cum Laude), where he earned the LFE Goldie

Award for Outstanding Scholarship, and was Managing Editor of the Syracuse Journal of International Law and Commerce.

His other published works include: *Bankruptcy Law - A Creditor's Perspective* (Lorman, 2004); *Bankruptcy Law - A Creditor's Perspective* (Lorman, 2001); *Real Assets in the Virtual World - An Introduction to eBusiness for Borrowers, Lenders, Trade Creditors and Their Counsel* (CBA, 2000); *Preparing For Disaster Before It Strikes* (NAPFA, 2000); *When Intellectual Property is not "Intellectual Property"* (CBA, 1998); *The Bankruptcy Chapter of the CBA's Basic Practice Manual* (CBA, 1994); *Techniques for Acquiring Undervalued Assets From Bankruptcy Estates* (CBA, 1993); *Setoffs Under Section 553 Of the United States Bankruptcy Code* (CBA, 1992); *Employment of Professionals Under Chapter 11 of the Bankruptcy Code* (CBA, 1992); and *Bankruptcy Law for the Corporate Lawyer* (CBA, 1989).

His seminars on bankruptcy law and business restructuring are highly regarded by business leaders, accountants and lawyers. His written commentaries on the United States Bankruptcy Code have appeared in Bankruptcy 360, The Connecticut Lawyer Magazine, The Wall Street Journal, the Connecticut Law Tribune and the New York Times. He lives in Connecticut with his wife and two sons.

*To my wife, Linda,
and our two sons, Myles and Brooks.*

Acknowledgments

I would like to express my appreciation and thanks to a number of people for their time and effort in the completion of this project: Lawrence Lipsher and Van Parker, financial and strategic advisors for their critical feedback; Katherine Brady, an associate attorney with Alderman & Alderman for her assistance with the footnotes; Brent Sampson, Chris Kline, John Draper, Jeanine and the entire team from Outskirts Press, that worked on this project for their support of this book; and Rosemarie Mahan for her assistance in managing the word processing of this manuscript.

Finally, I would like to express my appreciation to those friends, colleagues and family members who contributed to this project with their support, encouragement and instructive comments.

Myles H. Alderman, Jr.

Table of Contents

CHAPTER 1
Introduction

Each year tens of thousands of businesses ranging in size from small closely held companies to some of the largest corporations in the world respond to financial crisis by seeking to reorganize under Chapter 11 of the United States Bankruptcy Code. When they file, they bring with them into the bankruptcy process landlords and tenants, franchisors and franchisees, equipment lessors and lessees, intellectual property licensors and licensees, secured and unsecured creditors and a myriad of other parties in interest. Some Debtors emerge from bankruptcy with great success. Others fail miserably.

Further, what happens publicly in the United States Bankruptcy Courts is just a small fraction of the business workouts or business transactions influenced by

Chapter 11. For every business that restructures its debts using Chapter 11 of the United States Bankruptcy Code, there will be many others that restructure debts in out-of-court workouts. Although the parties to an out-of-court workout are not technically constrained by the requirements of the Bankruptcy Code, the decisions that are made and the final terms upon which they will agree are heavily influenced by what would happen in a Chapter 11 business reorganization or a Chapter 7 liquidation if the parties failed to reach an agreement.

The stakes in these workouts and Chapter 11 reorganizations are great. Businesses seek to reorganize under Chapter 11 because the Bankruptcy Code changes the rules under which businesses deal with their lenders, vendors, employees, landlords and others.

A successful reorganization can minimize losses for creditors, save jobs, preserve a customer for vendors and in some cases even preserve the equity for investors. However, the cost of restructuring and the impact on individual creditors can be substantial.

The process is complex and requires the skill and knowledge of trained bankruptcy professionals. To reorganize, debtors turn to lawyers, turnaround managers and accountants to help navigate the unique challenges of reorganizing under the Bankruptcy Code. The best of these professionals combine academic training, professional experience and strong business instincts. Secured lenders, vendors, landlords, licensors/licensees of intellectual property and other parties in interest can each benefit from solid legal counsel.

Unfortunately, only a small fraction of the companies that seek to reorganize under Chapter 11 actually succeed. In some cases, debtors have wasted precious resources on a Chapter 11 that was never feasible. Others could have feasibly reorganized, but made critical strategic mistakes early in the Chapter 11 process.

A successful Chapter 11 is one that returns to creditors an acceptable dividend on their claims and hopefully preserves a viable business. In a successful Chapter 11 business reorganization, the confirmed plan of reorganization will deliver a greater expected value for the reorganized business than would be available without the reorganization. For many constituents, the return on investment from participation in a successful reorganization can be very attractive.

A failed Chapter 11 case may be of no benefit to creditors, employees or vendors. To the contrary, a failed Chapter 11 may result in assets (that otherwise could have been deployed to limit the losses of creditors) being consumed by the costs of the Chapter 11 reorganization.

Success will be defined very differently for different stakeholders in a reorganization. One of my clients commented during a downdraft in the northeast real estate market in the late 1980's that "the easiest way to end up with a million dollars worth of commercial real estate is to start with ten million dollars in real estate." However, another client commented during the same economic cycle that the "best way to acquire ten million dollars worth of highly productive assets is to invest a couple million dollars into the acquisition of those assets from distressed companies in bankruptcy." Paradoxically, both could be correct.

From time to time, I am approached by a business leader who, after reading about the successful reorganization of another business, believes that his or her business should reorganize under Chapter 11. Some of these business leaders are correct that their companies can clearly benefit from a Chapter 11.

For example, a client in the aviation industry who operated a fixed base operation (think service station for airplanes) had a uniquely valuable piece of real estate that would have been lost without a Chapter 11. In that case, the client had a substantial facility on land leased to the debtor, pursuant to a lease under which the debtor had defaulted. With a Chapter 11, the debtor was able to cure the defaults, assume the lease and assign the lease to a buyer, thereby realizing a substantial recovery for the estate and its creditors. Without the Chapter 11, the debtor would have lost its interest in the leasehold.

Some of the alternatives to a Chapter 11 reorganization often include a surrender of assets to secured creditors, a liquidation under Chapter 7 or an out-of-court workout.

Practical & Tactical (Debtors)
Before deciding to file for protection from creditors under Chapter 11, the debtor should compare the probable outcomes under a Chapter 11 reorganization, a Chapter 7 liquidation and a surrender of assets to creditors and then explore whether a more favorable result can be obtained through an out-of-court workout.

This book cannot replace the benefits of good legal counsel, adequate funding or good pre-petition planning. However, armed with the information in this book you should be able to identify key issues and know the questions to ask your insolvency counsel.

This book is written for business leaders, accountants and

general counsel who may be called upon to work with bankruptcy attorneys in a Chapter 11 reorganization, or its alternatives, such as an out-of-court workout, on behalf of a debtor, a creditor, a party seeking to acquire assets from a debtor, or any other party in interest.

A Glossary of important terms used in this book starts on page 83. Section numbers refer to sections of the United States Bankruptcy Code. The full text of the Bankruptcy Code sections referred to in this book starts on page 95.

The Disclaimer: *This book is intended to provide general information. Actual legal advice is fact specific. Without knowing the facts of your situation, the author cannot provide you with appropriate legal advice. In addition, the law changes frequently, and may have changed since this book was written. The purchase of this book does not create an attorney-client relationship. DO NOT ACT, OR REFRAIN FROM ACTING, WITHOUT THE ADVICE OF COUNSEL.*

CHAPTER 2
Overview Of The Bankruptcy Code

Chapter 11 business reorganizations are subject to the statutory constraints of the United States Bankruptcy Code. The legislature was granted the authority to promulgate uniform bankruptcy laws by the First Article of the United States Constitution. Modern bankruptcy laws have evolved from laws regulating creditor-debtor relations that can be traced back to the beginning of written history. Over the years, reactions to insolvency have ranged from indentured servitude to debtors' prisons.

The term "bankrupt" dates back to the Roman Empire. During the Roman Empire, a merchant who could not pay his obligations to the empire was put out of business.

When this was done, the table in the bazaar from which he had conducted his business was broken. The word "Bankrupt" appears to come from the Latin word "bankus" meaning bench and "ruptus" meaning broken.

In the United States today, the Bankruptcy laws are designed to balance two competing goals: To provide debtors with a fresh start;[1] and to end the creditor's "race to the courthouse." [2]

The Bankruptcy Code is divided into nine chapters. With the exception of Chapter 12, the Bankruptcy Code only contains odd numbered chapters. Debtors can file for protection from creditors under chapters 7, 9, 11, 12, 13 or 15. Chapters 1, 3 and 5 apply to bankruptcies commenced under any chapter.

Chapter 1

Chapter 1 of the Bankruptcy Code contains definitions (§ 101), Rules of Construction (§ 102), and a description of the Powers of the Bankruptcy Court (§ 105).

Chapter 3

Chapter 3 of the Bankruptcy Code contains sections that apply to case administration, including: How cases are commenced; the debtor's relationships with its officers and professionals; and how cases are administered.

---

[1] *Grogan v. Garner*, 498 U.S. 279, 111 S.Ct. 289 (1915).
[2] *In re Bullion Reserve of North America*, 836 F. 2 1214 (9th Cir. 1988).

Chapter 5

Chapter 5 of the Bankruptcy Code defines the debtor's estate, creditors' claims against the estate, the priorities between various claims, and the pre-petition transfers that can be avoided by the debtor.

Chapter 7

Chapter 7 controls the process by which a debtor's assets are gathered and liquidated to pay the debtor's pre-petition debts. Chapter 7 is available to individuals and businesses. Individuals who qualify for Chapter 7 can obtain a discharge of their Pre-Petition debt while retaining their exempt assets (including a home and automobiles). Corporate debtors do not enjoy the benefit of asset exemptions.

Chapter 9

Chapter 9 defines the process by which a municipal debtor can adjust its debts. Because of the taxing authority available to municipalities, these cases are relatively rare.

Chapter 11

Chapter 11 defines the process by which a debtor engaged in business may reorganize. Chapter 11 plans may be based upon a reorganization of the business, a sale of the debtor's assets, a sale of the debtor's business as a going concern, or some combination of these options.

Chapter 12

Chapter 12 defines the process by which a family farmer with a regular income may adjust his/her/their debts pursuant to a plan based upon the farmer's future disposable income over a five-year period.

Chapter 13

Chapter 13 defines the process by which an individual (or husband and wife) with a regular income may adjust his/her/their debts pursuant to a plan based upon the debtor's future disposable income over a five-year period.

Chapter 15

Chapter 15 defines the process by which ancillary and other cross-border insolvency proceedings are handled.

> **Practical & Tactical**
> An understanding of how claims are treated under Chapter 11 and Chapter 7 is helpful for making decisions for an out-of-court workout of a business that could reorganize under Chapter 11. Chapters 9, 12, 13 and 15 are not available to business debtors.

CHAPTER 3
Parties To A Chapter 11

Chapter 11 cases are often large and complex. One of my cases has so many thousands of creditors that even the largest courtroom in the district could not accommodate all the attorneys who had a right to be heard on certain motions. Some motions in that case have resulted in hearings with so many parties that had a right to be heard that the courtroom was packed to standing room capacity with attorneys while dozens of other attorneys participated by joining onto the court's conference call.

Chart 1 shows a simplified view of the major types of interested parties in a Chapter 11 business reorganization.

Chart 1 - Parties

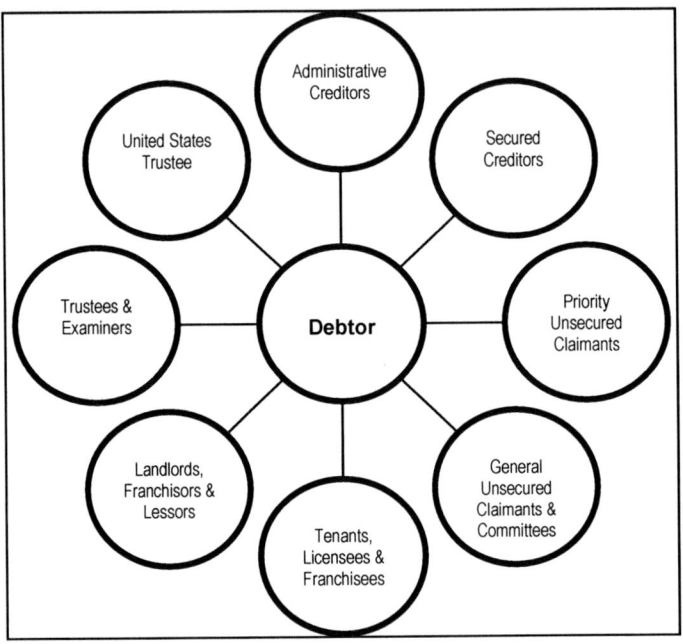

The Debtor

In a Chapter 11 business reorganization, the debtor is the business, or individual engaged in business, that is the subject of reorganization. The debtor may be a debtor-in-possession pursuant to sections 1107 and 1108 of the Bankruptcy Code. As the debtor-in-possession, a debtor has a fiduciary duty to its creditors.[3] To be eligible to be a debtor, the business or individual engaged in business must be insolvent on a balance sheet basis (total liabilities exceed total assets) or insolvent on a cash flow basis (unable to pay its current obligations as they come due).

---

[3] *See In re G-I Holdings, Inc.*, 385 F.3d 313 (3rd. cir. 2004).

A financially healthy company with no need to reorganize is not entitled to be a debtor under Chapter 11, and the courts will dismiss a Chapter 11 case filed by a "debtor" that does not need protection.[4]

Secured Creditors

Secured creditors are those claimants who hold allowed claims that are secured by validly perfected security interests in assets of the debtor to the extent of the value of the collateral securing their claims. See § 506(a).

Administrative Claimants

Administrative claimants are those claimants who are entitled to allowance of their fees and/or expenses for post-petition goods or services provided to the debtor.[5] Administrative claims enjoy a priority over almost all unsecured pre-petition claims. Each holder of an administrative claim must be paid in full, or upon such terms and conditions as it will accept, in order for a plan of reorganization to be confirmed.[6]

Priority Unsecured Creditors

Priority unsecured creditors are those claimants who hold allowed general unsecured claims, that are entitled to priority over general unsecured claims pursuant to § 507.

---

[4] *See In re SGL Carbon Corp.*, 200 F.3d 154 (3rd Cir. 1999).
[5] *See In re ITC Delta Comp., Inc.*, Case # 02-11848(MFW) (Del. 2006)
[6] See §§ 503 and 1129.

General Unsecured Creditors

General unsecured creditors are those claimants with allowed general unsecured claims for debts arising pre-petition.

Committees

To help ensure that the interests of general unsecured creditors are protected in a Chapter 11 case, the United States Trustee may appoint one or more committees of creditors generally made up of those seven creditors with the largest unsecured claims.[7] The creditors' committee represents the interests of all general unsecured creditors of the debtor. The role of the committee is to maximize the recovery for the entire class of unsecured creditors. The members of a creditors' committee and its counsel owe a fiduciary duty to holders of claims they are appointed to represent.[8]

The duties facing creditors' committee members are most challenging when there are multiple potential classes of creditors within the class that the committee has been appointed to represent. I recall one committee that represented the interests of people suffering from asbestosis as a result of years working for a debtor in one of its facilities that used asbestos. The challenge facing the committee was how to address the claims of those employees who were exposed to the asbestos, but who had not yet been symptomatic for asbestosis. In that case the conflicts between those who were exposed to asbestos and had symptoms of

---

[7] *See* 11 U.S.C. § 1102. *In re Oneida Ltd,* Case # 06-10489 (ALG) (Bankr. S.D.N.Y. May 4, 2006).
[8] *See In Re Refco,* 336 B.R. 187, 195 (Bankr. S.D.N.Y 2006).

asbestosis and those who had been exposed but had no symptoms were such that the formation of two separate committees was appropriate.

The Bankruptcy Abuse Prevention and Consumer Protection Act of 2005 contains in section 1102(b)(3) a new requirement for access to information for certain creditors. As of this writing it is too early to know how courts will address the problems created by this section. At least one court has already recognized that the application of this section will require the balancing of the competing interests of protecting confidential non-public or proprietary information against the right of parties to access to information. [9]

The creditors' committee can help ensure maximum recovery for the class of general unsecured creditors by consulting with the trustee or debtor-in-possession about the administration of the case, investigating the debtor-in-possession's operation of its business and participating in the formulation of a plan of reorganization. [10]

Landlords, Franchisors and Licensors

Landlords, franchisors and licensors each are parties to executory contracts with the debtor. Bankruptcy cases pose unique risks for parties to executory contracts. An entire book could be written on the issues facing each of these parties. However, the single most important common element is the power granted to the debtor-in-possession by section 365 of the Code. All parties to executory contracts with a debtor will benefit from an early analysis of contractual requirements and

---

[9] *Id.*
[10] See 11 U.S.C. § 1103.

consideration of modifications to the deadlines to assume or reject executory contracts.

Trustees and Examiners

In a Chapter 11 case, the debtor usually retains control of its property and management of its affairs. However, the Court can appoint a trustee to replace the debtor if there is sufficient evidence of fraud, dishonesty or incompetence.[11] In cases in which there is sufficient evidence to raise a question, but insufficient evidence to prove actual fraud, dishonesty or incompetence, the court may appoint an examiner, who has authority to examine the debtor's affairs, while allowing the debtor to retain control.[12] In most cases the person appointed to act as the trustee in a case will be an individual in private practice who is selected for his/her integrity and competence in dealing with difficult bankruptcy related issues. An appointed trustee is separate and distinct from the United States Trustee Program.

The United States Trustee

The office of the United States Trustee is a division of the Department of Justice. An attorney from the office of the United States Trustee supervises the administration of a case and ensures that the bankruptcy laws are upheld. In a Chapter 11, duties of the U.S. Trustee include: reviewing debtor's requests for emergency orders, establishing committees, reviewing reorganization plans and disclosure statements, ensuring timely filing of reports, schedules and fees, and reviewing applications to employ.

---

[11] See § 1104.
[12] See 11 U.S.C. §§ 1106 1107.

> **Practical & Tactical**
> During the course of a Chapter 11 case, parties that have adverse interests on a motion may well be aligned with common interests on other aspects of the case. Do not underestimate the importance of understanding the objectives and agendas of major constituents to a case and developing good working relationships.

Type of Claims and Their Priorities

As a general rule, claims in a bankruptcy case are not entitled to any payment unless the claims ahead of them are paid in full, or on such terms as are acceptable to The holders of prior claims. [13]

The relative priority of claims is prescribed by section 507 of the United States Bankruptcy Code. In defining priorities, the Code's focus is on allowed claims. Not every claim against a debtor will be an allowed claim. Claims listed by the debtor on its schedules as undisputed and liquidated will be deemed allowed.

Further, claims alleged by a timely filed proof of claim filed in accordance with Section 501 will be allowed if no objection is interposed.[14] If an objection to a proof of claim is filed, the court will determine the extent to which the claim is allowed after a properly noticed hearing. [15]

Unfortunately, on many occasions I have witnessed a holder of an otherwise unimpeachable large claim,

---

[13] See 11 U.S.C. § 507.

[14] § 502(a); *In re Oakwood Homes Corp.*, 05-2-32 (3d Cir., 2006).

[15] § 502(b).

compelled to accept less then its fair share of the distribution in a Chapter 11 because its counsel failed to file a proper proof of claim in a timely manner. I have seen these claimants allege excusable neglect pursuant to Rule 9006 or claim that some prior written communication or pleading constituted an Informal Proof of Claim to mitigate the damage – Usually with the result of a compromise that allows the claim for a fraction of the full claim.

An allowed claim is one that has been filed by a creditor, or listed by the debtor, to which no objection has been interposed. A disputed claim is a claim to which an objection has been raised that has not been resolved, and a disallowed claim is a claim to which an objection has been filed and which has been ordered disallowed by the Bankruptcy Court.

Allowed claims are entitled to priority in accordance with Section 507. Chart 2 depicts the major prioritization of claims.

Chart 2
Priorities

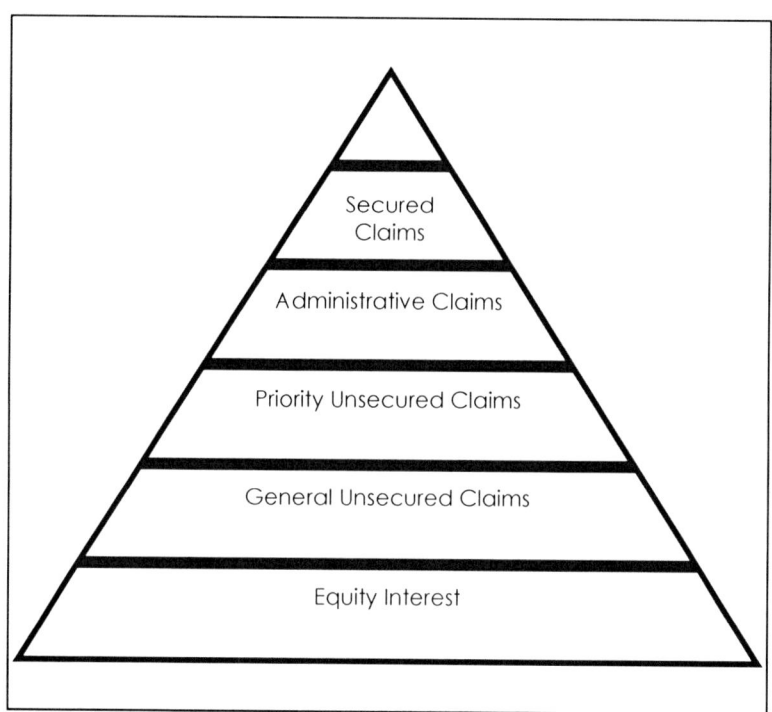

Secured Claims

Secured claims are those claims that are protected by a validly perfected security interest in assets of the debtor to the extent of the value of the collateral securing their claims.[16] Generally, the Bankruptcy Code does not deprive the holder of validly perfected secured claims and thus, secured claims are paid before other creditors. However, secured claims are subject to attack under the Bankruptcy Code in ways not available to debtors or

---

[16] See 11 U.S.C. § 506.

other creditors outside of bankruptcy. This important issue is addressed in further detail in the discussion of avoidance actions in Chapter 5.

Administrative Expenses

Administrative expenses are the expenses and costs of operating the debtor in bankruptcy. After notice and hearing, the court will allow the actual and necessary costs and expenses of preserving the estate as administrative expenses.[17] Administrative expenses include allowed compensation to professionals.[18]

Additionally, administrative expenses include the actual and necessary costs and expenses of preserving assets for the benefit of a secured claimant. This expense may be recovered from the property securing an allowed claim. [19]

It is not uncommon for substantial disputes to arise over the issue of what costs and expenses are necessary to preserve an asset for the benefit of a creditor. In one case, my client had a license to use certain critical intellectual property, subject to a "no interruption in service" restriction. Without the protection of a Chapter 11, creditors could have forced an interruption in services and the debtor would have risked the loss of its critically valuable license. Through the use of Chapter 11 the debtor was able to assume and assign this critical intellectual property. If a Chapter 11 business reorganization was required to protect the value of this business, how much of the Chapter 11 expenses could

---

[17] See 11 U.S.C. § 503. *In re Eagle-Picher Industries, Inc.*, 04-3747 (6th Cir., 2006).
[18] See §§ 330 and 331.
[19] See § 506(c).

rightly be charged to the lender pursuant to section 506(c)? In that case, the court was not required to decide the issue because we succeeded in persuading the secured lender to agree to pay for all the costs of the Chapter 11 reorganization.

Priority Unsecured Claims

Priority unsecured claims are those allowed unsecured claims that are entitled to priority over other unsecured creditors pursuant to section 507. For the full list, consult Section 507. Priority claims that are most likely to be encountered in a Chapter 11 business reorganization are:

A. Wage claims up to $10,000;
B. Sales commissions;
C. Claims for pre-petition employee benefits up to $10,000;
D. Farmer and fisherman;
E. Consumer deposits up to a sum certain; and
F. Certain tax claims. [20]

General Unsecured Claims

General unsecured claims are those claims for which there is no collateral securing the claimant's interest and which are not entitled to priority pursuant to Section 507. After all priority claims are paid in full, general unsecured claimants will be paid their *pro rata share* of remaining assets.

---

[20] See §§ 330 and 331.

Equity Security Interests

An equity security holder is a holder of an equity security of the debtor such as a share in a corporation, an interest of a limited partner in a limited partnership, or a right to purchase, sell, or subscribe to a share, security, or interest of a share in a corporation or an interest in a limited partnership.[21] An equity security holder may vote on the plan of reorganization and may file a proof of interest. Equity security holders are not entitled to any dividend or continuing interest unless the allowed claims entitled to priority are paid in full, or on such other terms as they will agree to accept.

Practical & Tactical
85% of $100 is worth more than 100% of $70. Parties with superior claims have the legal right to demand payment in full before subordinate claims are paid. However, holders of all allowed claims have the right to object to the confirmation of a plan of reorganization and the holders of allowed claims not being paid in full have the right to vote to oppose confirmation. If a proposed plan will significantly increase the size of the pot of money to be distributed, a creditor with a superior right to payment might agree to give up a percentage of its right to money to share with a subordinate class in order to get a plan confirmed.

---

[21] See 11 U.S.C. 101(16).

CHAPTER 4
Operating The Debtor-In-Possession

Commencement of the Case

A Chapter 11 business reorganization can be commenced either by a voluntary petition filed by the debtor or by an involuntary petition filed against the debtor.

Voluntary Petition

A Chapter 11 business reorganization can be commenced by the filing of a voluntary petition along with a list of the twenty largest unsecured creditors, an abbreviated balance sheet, a "matrix" with the name and address of every creditor and evidence of proper authority to commence the case.[22]

Throughout the Bankruptcy Code, the date of the filing of the voluntary petition is referred to as the "Petition Date" and the filing of the voluntary petition is referred to as the "order for relief."

The process by which the debtor obtains authority to file the voluntary petition is similar to the process by which the business governance body would take any other substantial legal action on behalf of the business. If it is a corporation, appropriate steps will have to be taken to obtain the necessary approval and authority of the company's board of directors.

Involuntary Petition

A Chapter 11 case can also be commenced by creditors of a debtor through the use of an Involuntary Petition.[23] The primary reason that creditors are likely to seek an involuntary petition is if they suspect fraud and/or incompetence at a level that they believe is increasing the risk of financial loss with the passage of time.

Three or more holders of unsecured claims of $10,000 or more that are not contingent or subject to *bona fide* dispute may file an involuntary petition against a debtor that is not generally paying its debts as they come due.[24] If the debtor has less than twelve creditors, then one

---

[22] See 11 U.S.C. § 301.
[23] See 11 U.S.C. § 303. *See In re Demirco Holdings, Inc.*, 06-70122 (Bankr., C.D. Ill, 2006).
[24] See 11 U.S.C. § 303(b)(1).

creditor can commence an involuntary bankruptcy.[25] Filing an involuntary petition without the requisite number of holders of unsecured claims that are free from *bona fide* dispute exposes the filer to substantial penalty.[26] As an example, in a recent case a debtor recovered more than $6,000,000 from a creditor that was found to have improperly filed an Involuntary Petition.[27]

Chapter 11 Timeline

There are many dates that are important to the legal analysis of the Chapter 11 reorganization process. Some will be set by the court during the reorganization, others are proscribed by statute. The timeline that follows identifies some of the important dates in a typical Chapter 11 reorganization.

4 Years Pre-Petition -
- Transfers made after this date, that can be shown to be fraudulent pursuant to the Uniform Fraudulent Transfer Act may be avoided. See § 544.

2 Years Pre-Petition –
- Transfers made after this date for which there was inadequate consideration, or which involved actual fraud may be avoided. See § 548.

1 Year Pre-Petition –
- Transfers from the debtor to insiders made after this date may be subject to avoidance as preferential transfers. See § 547.

90 Days Pre Petition –
- Transfers from the debtor to unsecured creditors

---

[25] See, 11 U.S.C. § 303(b)(2).
[26] See, 11 U.S.C. § 303(i).
[27] *In Re John Richard Holmes Building Co., LLC* 04-2154 (6th Cir., 2006).

made after this date may be subject to avoidance as Preferential Transfers. See § 547.

45 Days Pre-Petition –
- Goods delivered after this date may be subject to a valid reclamation claim.

Petition Date

15 Days Post-Petition –
- Deadline to file complete schedules.

20 Days Post-Petition –
- Utility companies may terminate service if they have not been provided adequate assurance of payment. See § 366.

Reasonable Time After Filing (often first 45 days) –
- Initial meeting of creditors pursuant to Section 341.

Time set by Court –
- Bar Date for filing proofs of claims. Untimely proofs of claims will not be allowed, absent a showing an excusable neglect. See § 501.

120 Days Post-Petition
- Debtor's exclusive period to file a plan of reorganization expires unless plan has been filed or time has been increased or decreased by the court.
- Debtor is deemed to have rejected unexpired non-residential leases that have not been assumed, unless the time to assume or reject has been extended by the court. See § 365.
- Debtor's professionals may seek allowance of fees and expenses once every 120 days, unless the court authorizes a different frequency. See § 331.

180 Days Post-Petition –
- If the debtor filed its plan of reorganization within 120 days of the Petition date, but fails to have the plan confirmed by this date, its exclusive period to file a plan ends, unless increased or decreased by the court.

Effect of Commencement

Upon the filing of the petition, the business becomes a debtor-in-possession. It is helpful to imagine the debtor-in-possession as a new entity that has a duty to pay its post-petition obligations as they come due. The debtor-in-possession should strive to emerge from bankruptcy with a confirmed plan of reorganization that will provide some form of payment to its pre-petition creditors. Unlike the pre-petition debtor, the debtor-in-possession has a statutory fiduciary[28] duty to its creditors, will have substantial new reporting and operating requirements and will need to obtain court authority for many business decisions.

The United States Trustee also conducts a meeting of creditors, called the "341 meeting."[29] This meeting of creditors generally occurs about a month after filing the petition and is an opportunity for the creditors and United States Trustee to inquire about the debtor's assets and liabilities and to verify the accuracy of the debtor's schedules.

Debtor's Duties Upon Filing

The following is a sample of some of the steps that a debtor is required to take upon filing of a petition for reorganization.

- Close its pre-petition bank accounts.
- Advise the bank(s) with pre-petition accounts of the Chapter 11 filing and instruct them not to

---

[28] *In re Ford Motor Credit Co. v. Weaver*, 680 F.2d 451, 462 (6th Cir. 1982).
[29] See 11 U.S.C. § 341.

honor checks against the pre-petition account(s).

- New accounts must be established at an institution on the U.S. Trustee's list of approved institutions.
- Separate accounts must be opened for operating account(s) and the debtor's tax account(s).
- Checks for the operating account should be printed with "Debtor-In-Possession" or "D-I-P" after the debtor's name and must have the bankruptcy case number.
- Checks for the tax account must be printed with "D-I-P, TAX ACCOUNT" and the case number.
- All insurance policies must be changed to cover the interest of the debtor as debtor-in-possession.
- Absolutely no payments for pre-petition obligations should be made (except pursuant to court order).
- Arrangements must be made with utility companies to set up new post-petition accounts with appropriate deposits as adequate assurance of payments pursuant to section 366.

Additional Issues For Debtor's Management To Attend To After Filing For Protection Under Chapter 11:

- Unless an extension of deadlines has been obtained, Schedules must be completed and filed with the Bankruptcy Court within ten days of filing.
- Monthly operating reports (financial statements) are due by the fifteenth of each month. Accountants with an understanding of the requirements of a Chapter 11 case should be retained to assist with these reports and the other duties of a debtor-in-possession because of the unique and complex nature of these reporting requirements.
- As a general rule, fees may not be paid for

professional services of any kind without an order authorizing the employment of that professional and order authorizing the payment.

- Distributions may not be paid to any insiders other than ordinary W-2 salary.
- Neither an attorney nor an accountant is authorized to render any professional services to the debtor-in-possession without an appropriate application to the court and approval thereof.
- All accountants for the company should be notified immediately of the filing of the Chapter 11. The books of the company shall be closed as of the petition date and new books opened for the debtor-in-possession as of the petition date.
- For tax and other purposes, the debtor-in-possession must be considered a new entity.
- If the company will be issuing any W-2 payroll, the Internal Revenue Service should be communicated with in order to establish new payroll withholding accounts.
- While the company may extend credit in the ordinary course to customers, credit should not be extended to insiders or employees. Somewhat higher care should be used when extending credit to customers, because some customers are slower to pay, or completely fail to pay, obligations to companies in Chapter 11.

Practical & Tactical (Debtors)

A business bankruptcy filing should be accompanied by an appropriate public relations strategy. A company's filing for protection from creditors is usually a news worthy story. Without proper media relations, the filing of a petition could trigger a story that reads "[Your Debtor's Name] Declares Bankruptcy" with a story that can harm both sales and the prospects for reorganization. With a well-conceived factual press release, the headline can become "[Your Debtor's Name] To Reorganize To Improve Productivity With New Funding From [DIP Lender].

Should any creditor also be a customer, it is improper for such creditor/customer to offset post-petition obligations to the debtor against its pre-petition claims against the debtor.

Any property of the debtor which is in the hands of third parties, whether deposits to utilities, tooling, or the like, is subject to the jurisdiction of the Bankruptcy Court, and may not be applied or appropriated or used by the third party once the filing has occurred. (However, consigned inventory in the hands of third parties can be used in the ordinary course of business.) Under appropriate circumstances, an order of turnover may be obtained with respect to tooling, or other tangible personal property. However, the party holding a deposit may apply to the court for the right to set-off.

Property of the Estate

The property of the estate includes all of the debtor's legal and equitable interests in property as of the petition date.[30] This includes, for example, tangible assets, claims against third parties, and patents. Anyone holding property on behalf of the debtor must turn that property over to the debtor. Moreover, any property that the trustee recovers using its avoidance powers (discussed in Chapter 5) becomes property of the estate.

The Automatic Stay

The commencement of a bankruptcy case automatically stays a wide range of actions against the debtor.[31] The automatic stay is designed to prevent a creditors' race to the courthouse and provide the debtor with a period of time to reorganize its affairs. As a general rule, actions to collect money or enforce contract rights are stayed. The automatic stay does not apply to governmental actions designed to protect public health and safety.[32] With the most recent revisions to the Bankruptcy Code, a number of other actions related to domestic (family) support obligations or the rights of certain secured lenders are also exempted from the automatic stay. It should be noted that the exceptions are substantial. For a complete list of what is stayed, see Section 362 of the Bankruptcy Code.

A creditor is entitled to relief from the automatic stay for cause, including a lack of adequate protection if the debtor does not have an equity interest in the property and the property is not necessary for an effective

---

[30] See 11 U.S.C. 541; *In re Bean*, 252 F.3d 113 (2d. Cir. 20010); *In re Mid-Island Hosp.* Inc., 276 F.3d 123 (2d. Cir., 2002).
[31] See 11 U.S.C. § 362(d); *In re Bevilacque*, 05-34188 (Bankr. ED.Pa, 2006).
[32] See 11 U.S.C. § 362(b)(4); *In re Ngan Gung Restaurant, Inc.*, 183 B.R. 689 (Bankr S.D.N.Y. 1995); *In re IT Group, Inc., Co.*, 02-10118 (MFW) (Bankr. D.Del. 2006).

reorganization; or if the debtor fails to file a plan of reorganization with a "reasonable possibility of being confirmed within a reasonable time" in a single asset real estate case.[33]

Practical & Tactical (Creditors)

When in doubt as to whether a contemplated action is stayed by the automatic stay contained in Section 362, the best practice is to consult with counsel to determine whether a motion for relief from the automatic stay is required.

Practical & Tactical (Debtors)

If a creditor is initiating or continuing actions that appear to be a violation of the automatic stay, the best practice is to consult with counsel to determine whether an action is required to cause the creditor to honor the automatic stay To assist in enforcement of the automatic stay, the debtor should make sure that its lead bankruptcy counsel has a list of all pending legal matters to which the debtor is a party.

Financing Considerations

A Chapter 11 debtor will require operating capital. Therefore, most debtors will need to move for authority to use cash collateral pursuant to section 363 or to borrow money pursuant to section 364.

---

[33] See 11 U.S.C. 362(d).

Use of Cash Collateral

Lenders that have a security interest in the debtor's assets also have a security interest in the proceeds, products, offspring, rents and profits derived from those assets. Those proceeds are known as "cash collateral." A debtor may not use cash collateral, without the consent of the secured party or a court order authorizing its use. [34]

D-I-P Financing

Debtors who need more money than is available as cash collateral may also need to borrow money post-petition. Debtors are obligated to seek financing on the most favorable terms available. Debtors who are unable to borrow money on more favorable terms, may offer a lender a post-petition security interest and a super priority over other claims, even over allowed administrative claims.[35]

---

[34] See § 363; *Unsecured Creditors' Committee v. Jones Truck Lines*, 156 B.R. 608 (Bankr. W.D. Ark, 1992); *In re Enron Corp.*, 02-3702 (RCC), (S.D.N.Y, 2006).
[35] See § 364; *In re Kmart Corp.*, 02-B-02474 (Bankr. N.D.Ill., 2006).

Practical & Tactical (Creditors)

A secured creditor who consents to the use of its cash collateral without requiring adequate protection (such as replacement liens) cannot be given additional collateral or super-priority claims that might have been available had it refused to authorize the use of cash collateral without such protection. Similarly, a lender offering debtor-in-possession financing who agrees to lend without post-petition collateral or super priority claims cannot be given that collateral or super priority claims that might have been available had it refused to fund without such protection. Accordingly, lenders should be careful to demand as much as they need to protect themselves under Sections 363 and 364.

Ordinary Course Transactions

While operating as a debtor-in-possession, a business may continue to operate and conduct its business by engaging in ordinary course transactions. The debtor may use, sell or lease property of the estate, other than cash collateral, in the ordinary course.[36]

Use, Sale and Leases Outside The Ordinary Course

The debtor may not engage in transactions outside the ordinary course without an appropriate court order.[37] A court may issue an order authorizing the use, sale or lease outside the ordinary course after a properly

---

[36] See 11 U.S.C. § 1108; *In re Lodge America*, 259 B.R. 728 (Bankr. D.Kan. (2001).

[37] See 11 U.S.C. § 364.

noticed hearing on the debtor's motion. [38]

What is ordinary course depends upon the business. If there is any doubt as to whether a certain transaction is outside the ordinary course, debtor's management should consult with its bankruptcy counsel to determine whether an application for authority is required.

Sales Free and Clear of Interest

The debtor may sell its property free and clear of the interests of others with an interest in that property (such as secured claims) with an appropriate court order. Pursuant to section 363(f), the court should issue an order authorizing the debtor to sell property free and clear of any interests of others in that property only if: (1) applicable non-bankruptcy law permits sale of such property free and clear of such interest; (2) such entity consents; (3) such interest is a lien and the price at which such property is to be sold is greater than the aggregate value of all liens on such property; (4) such interest in *bona fide* dispute; or (5) such entity could be compelled, in a legal or equitable proceeding, to accept a money satisfaction of such interest.[39]

Once a section 363 sale has been consummated in good faith by a purchaser, the transfer will survive even if the original court order approving the sale is reversed on appeal.[40]

---

[38] See 11 U.S.C. § 364(b).

[39] See 11 U.S.C. § 363(f); *In re 3-D Cash & Carry, Inc.* 04-80098 (DHW) (Bankr M.D. Ala., 2006).

[40] See § 363(m).

One of my clients is particularly astute at identifying undervalued intellectual property and has worked with us to acquire intellectual property assets from debtors. Transactions structured as section 363 sales and acquisitions that can be completed with sufficient speed and efficiency minimize the risks associated with acquiring the target assets from a debtor in bankruptcy. The speed of the transactions helps keep the transactional costs down while minimizing the risks associated with the deals. In one case a client recovered the entire cost of an asset acquisition from the cash-flow from the acquired assets in just nine months following acquisition.

Practical & Tactical

Valuations of property of the estate are important evidence for a number of calculations, including: The debtor's right to sell property free and clear pursuant to section 363(3); A creditor's right to relief from stay and/or adequate protection pursuant to section 362(d); and a secured creditor's right to interest and/or legal fees. The interplay between the various motions that may be filed and the conflicting evidentiary needs for each should be carefully analyzed before any of these motions are filed or appraisals commissioned.

Executory Contracts

A contract is executory if there is something left to be done by both of the parties to the transaction. Examples of executory contracts include leases (of both real and personal property) and contracts for continued use of a license or franchise.

Assumption and Rejection

The Bankruptcy Code allows the debtor (not the creditor) to either assume or reject an executory contract.[41] When the debtor assumes the contract it is obligated to cure any defaults under that contract (including the payment of any arrearages).[42] If the debtor rejects the contract, then the damages to which the other party would be entitled as a result of that breach are treated as an unsecured claim as of the petition date.

An executory contract may not be assumed if it was properly terminated prior to the petition date. However, *ipso facto* clauses that purport to terminate a contract or lease upon the debtor's filing for bankruptcy merely because of that filing are void as against public policy.[43]

From time to time, companies that are restructuring under Chapter 11 are themselves creditors of other companies that are also debtors under separate Chapter 11 cases. In a number of these cases, it is the filing for bankruptcy by a major business customer that causes another business to need to seek protection from its creditors.

Several years ago the filing for Chapter 11 reorganization by two companies that were parties to an executory contract could have caused two Bankruptcy Courts in

---

[41] See 11 U.S.C. § 365; *National Labor Relations Board v. Bildisco & Bildisco*, 465 U.S. 513 (1984); *In re Ionosphere Clubs, Inc.*, 85 F.3d 992 (2d Cir., 1996); *In re Access Beyond Technologies, Inc.* 237 B.R. 32 (Bankr. Del., 1999); *In re Chateaugay Corp.*, 10 F3d 944 (2d Cir. 1993).

[42] *In re New Breed Realty Enterprises, Inc.* 278 B.R. 314 (Bankr. E.D.N.Y. 2002).

[43] See 11 U.S.C. 365(e)(1); *In re C.A.F. Bindery, Inc.*, 199 B.R. 828 (Bankr. S.D.N.Y., 1996).

two different jurisdictions to address the question: "If the debtor in a Chapter 11 has the exclusive right to assume or reject an executory contract, what happens if both parties are debtors and each sought an order in its case for assumption or rejection of the contract?" The contract in question was for "mission critical" information technology ("I.T.") support services to a national retailer. The retailer was operating under a Chapter 11 in the Southern District of New York. The I.T. company was operating under Chapter 11 in the District of Connecticut. Rather than run the risk of a catastrophic adverse ruling from the bankruptcy case of the other party, the two debtors reached a compromise that allowed the retailer access to the mission critical services it needed, while affording the I.T. Company the contract modifications that it needed for its Chapter 11.

Assignment

A debtor that has assumed an executory contract under section 365 may assign that executory contract to a third party. The debtor may assign a previously assumed executory contract or unexpired lease if the assignee provides adequate assurance of future performance.[44] The assignee must provide this assurance whether or not there has been a default in such contract or lease. Once a debtor properly assigns an executory contract or unexpired lease, it is no longer obligated under that agreement.

Shopping Center Leases

When the executory contract is an unexpired lease of real estate located in a shopping center, the Bankruptcy

---

[44] See 11 U.S.C. § 365(b)(1).

Code requires a more specific showing of adequate assurance in order to assume or assign the contract.[45] In the case of a shopping center lease, adequate assurance includes a showing:

(1) of the source of rent and other consideration;
(2) that the percentage of rent due under such lease will not decline substantially;
(3) that assumption or assignment of such lease is subject to the provisions of section 365; and that assumption or assignment of the lease will not disrupt any tenant mix or balance in the shopping center.

Practical & Tactical

Until such a time as the debtor assumes or rejects its leases and other executory contracts, the debtor does not need to, and does not have authority to pay pre-petition debts related to the executory contract. However, with regard to unexpired leases of nonresidential real estate the debtor must timely perform all post-petition obligations under the lease (including the payment of post-petition rent).

Burdensome executory contracts should be rejected and executory contracts with benefit for the debtor should be assumed.

A landlord should be put on notice as of the petition date upon which its tenant becomes a debtor-in-possession.

---

[45] See 11 U.S.C. § 365(b)(3); *In re Ames Dept. Stores, Inc.*, 127 B.R. 744 (Bankr., S.D.N.Y. 1991).

CHAPTER 5
Avoidance Actions

The Bankruptcy Code gives the bankruptcy trustee (or debtor-in-possession) the power to avoid certain transfers of property.[46] Sections 544 and 548 allow the debtor-in-possession to avoid fraudulent transfers, while section 547 allows the debtor-in-possession to avoid preferential transfers. The debtor-in-possession takes on the rights of a lien creditor and *bona fide* purchaser, and can avoid those transfers that are voidable by lien creditors and *bona fide* purchasers.[47]

The debtor-in-possession may look to both bankruptcy

---

[46] See 11 U.S.C. §§ 544, 547, 548.
[47] See *U.S. v. Webster*, 125 F.3d 1024 (7th Cir. 1997); *Matter of Smith*, 966 F.2d 1527 (7th Cir. 1992).

law and non-bankruptcy law such as the Uniform Fraudulent Transfer Act to determine what transfers are voidable.

If a transferee of an avoidable transfer will not return what was transferred by the debtor then the debtor-in-possession may bring an adversary proceeding to have the transfer avoided and the property returned to the estate.

Preferential Transfers

Preferential transfers are voidable pursuant to Section 547.[48]

A transfer of property of the debtor is preferential if it is

1. made to, or for the benefit, of a creditor;
2. for, or on account of, an antecedent debt owed by the debtor to the creditor before the transfer;
3. made while the debtor was insolvent;
4. made
   - on or within 90 days before the petition date (One year if the transferee is an insider); or
5. a transfer that enables that creditor to receive more than it would have received if
   - the case were a case under a Chapter 7 liquidation;
   - the transfer had not been made; and
   - such creditor received payment of such debt to the extent provided by the provisions of this code.

---

[48] *See Union Bank v. Wolas*, 502 U.S. 151, 112 S.Ct. 527, 116 L.Ed. 2d 514 (1991); *In re Suffola, Inc.*, 2 F.3d 977 (9th Cir. 1993).

However, the Bankruptcy Code provides a safe harbor for transfers, or payments, for which there is contemporaneous exchange of new value[49] or that is made in the ordinary course of business.[50] A transfer qualifies as a contemporaneous exchange for new value where the parties contemplate and facilitate a near simultaneous transfer <u>and</u> where the value given to the creditor is equal to the value given to the debtor.[51]

A debtor's transfer is in the ordinary course where the debtor makes that transfer in payment of a debt incurred in the ordinary course of business <u>and</u> either made in accordance with the existing business relationship between the creditor and debtor <u>or</u> made according to general industry standards.[52]

Fraudulent Transfers

The Bankruptcy Code also gives the debtor-in-possession the power to avoid fraudulent transfers made within the year prior to the debtor filing bankruptcy.[53] The debtor-in-possession can look to both the Bankruptcy Code and non-bankruptcy law to determine what transfers can be avoided as fraudulent transfers.

Under the Bankruptcy Code, a fraudulent transfer occurs

---

[49] See 11 U.S.C. § 547 (c)(1); *In re JWJ Contracting Co., Inc.*, 371 F.3d 1079 (9th Cir. 2004).
[50] See 11 U.S.C. 547(c)(2); *In re Isaac Leaseco, Inc.*, 389 F.3d 1205 (11th Cir. 2004).
[51] See 11 U.S.C. § 547(c)(1).
[52] See 11 U.S.C. 547(c)(2); *In re National Steel Co.*, 341 B.R. 229 (Bankr.N.D.Ill. 2006).
[53] See 11 U.S.C. § 548; *In re Anderson*, 166 B.R. 516 (Bankr.D.Conn. 1994).

when there has been actual fraud[54] or constructive fraud.[55]

Actual fraud occurs when the debtor intentionally transfers property or incurs an obligation with the intent to hinder, delay or defraud its creditors.[56]

Constructive fraud occurs when the debtor receives less than a reasonably equivalent value in exchange for a transfer of property or its incurring an obligation and the debtor was insolvent or became insolvent as a result of the transfer. Constructive fraud also occurs when the debtor is engaged in a business for which the remaining capital is unreasonably small or where the debtor intended to incur debts beyond its ability to repay.[57]

The debtor-in-possession can recover these fraudulent transfers for the benefit of the bankruptcy estate when the transfer occurred within one year of the filing of the petition date.

The debtor-in-possession may also look to the Uniform Fraudulent Transfer Act (UFTA) as adopted by the state whose law controls to avoid fraudulent transfers.[58] Under UFTA, many fraudulent transfers can be avoided. Pursuant to UFTA, the debtor-in-possession can recover fraudulent transfers dating back four years.[59]

---

[54] See 11 U.S.C. § 548(a)(1)(A).
[55] See 11 U.S.C. § 548(a)(1)(B).
[56] See 11 U.S.C. § 548(a)(1)(A).
[57] See 11 U.S.C. § 548(a)(1)(B).
[58] See 52 Conn. Gen. Stat. § 552; *Dietter v. Dietter*, 54 Conn. App. 481, 737 A.2d 926 (1999).
[59] See 52 Conn. Gen. Stat. § 552j.

Practical & Tactical

Avoided transfers (both preferential and fraudulent) can provide a huge source of funding for administrative costs and/or distributions to creditors. The disgorgement of payments and transfers deemed to be fraudulent or preferential can range from an annoyance to a catastrophic loss. The manner in which pre-petition transactions are structured and documented can have an enormous impact on whether those transactions will survive an attack as either a fraudulent or preferential transfer. The cost of having a seasoned bankruptcy professional help structure transactions is nominal compared to the cost of defending an adversary proceeding after a debtor demands that a transfer be avoided.

CHAPTER 6
Issues Related To Secured Claims

A creditor's claim against a debtor is a secured claim to the extent that there is a validly perfected security interest in property of the estate.

Interest and Legal Fees

If the secured creditor's claim is over-secured (secured by assets worth more than the secured claim), the creditor is entitled to interest and legal fees.[60] A secured

---

[60] See 11 U.S.C. § 506(b); *In re Coney Island Amusement, Inc.*, 05 Civ. 08238 (LBS) (S.D.N.Y. March 13 2006).

creditor who is over-secured will most likely be afforded adequate protection by an equity cushion in its collateral and will not need cash payments, replacement liens or other relief such as super priority administrative claims.

Adequate Protection and Relief From Stay

Adequate Protection

A secured creditor is entitled to adequate protection against the diminution in the value of its collateral.[61]

Adequate protection may be provided in the form of cash payments, replacement liens on the other assets of the estate or other relief such as super priority administrative claims.

The debtor must offer some measure of protection that the value of the secured party's collateral will not decrease or otherwise be impaired. To protect the secured party's interest, the debtor may offer replacement liens or periodic cash payments.[62]

Lack of adequate protection may form the basis for:

   (1) A secured creditor's motion for relief from stay; [63] or
   (2) A secured creditor's opposition to the debtor's use

---

[61] See 11 U.S.C. § 361; *In re Gasel Transportation Lines, Inc.*, 326 B.R. 683 (6th Cir. 2005).
[62] See 11 U.S.C. § 361(1) and (2); *In re Westpoint Stevens, Inc.*, No. 05 Civ. 06860 (LTS) (S.D.N.Y. November 16 2005).
[63] See 11 U.S.C. § 362(d)(1).

of cash collateral; [64] or

(3) A secured creditor's opposition to a borrowing motion. [65]

Relief from the Automatic Stay

A creditor may move for relief from the automatic stay for cause, including a lack of adequate protection. Relief from the automatic stay may be granted to recover property if the debtor does not have an equity interest in the property and the property is not necessary for an effective reorganization. With regard to a single asset real estate case, relief from the automatic stay may also be granted if the debtor fails to file a plan of reorganization with a "reasonable possibility of being confirmed within a reasonable time."[66]

Setoff

The Bankruptcy Code preserves many, but not all, aspects of non-bankruptcy setoff rights.[67] In the context of a bankruptcy case, the mutual debts in question must have ripened pre-petition. A creditor cannot setoff a post-petition obligation against a pre-petition claim.

For a debt to be mutual both claims must be valid, fully matured, and of the same right. For example, a tenant may not set off a negligence claim against a rent

---

[64] See 11 U.S.C. § 363(e).

[65] See 11 U.S.C. § 364(d).

[66] See 11 U.S.C. 362(d); *In re Oligbo*, Case No. 02-26161-ess; Adv. Pro. No. 04-1037-ess (Bankr.E.D.N.Y. March 30, 2005).

[67] See 11 U.S.C. § 553; *In re Hudson*, Case No. 00-11683 (Bankr.N.D.N.Y. May 16 2006).

claim.[68] Bankruptcy courts also require mutuality of the parties: the party with the claim against the debtor must be the same party against whom the debtor has a claim. Therefore, affiliated corporations may not aggregate their claims.[69]

A creditor seeking to enforce a setoff right in bankruptcy must first obtain relief from the automatic stay. A setoff claim is a secured claim under the Bankruptcy Code.[70] Because of its secured status, a setoff claim may be entitled to adequate protection as described above.

The Code imposes several limitations on setoff rights. The Code prohibits creditors from trafficking claims to create offsetting obligations.[71] The Bankruptcy Court will not allow a setoff where a creditor deceptively accepted or obtained deposits with the intent of applying them to a preexisting claim.[72] In addition, the general rules applying to preferences (detailed above) also apply to setoff rights that meet the definition of a preference.[73] If a creditor's pre-petition setoff results in an improved position compared to the position the creditor would have been in had it waited until the petition date, the setoff may be set aside.[74]

---

[68] See *In re Becker Bros.*, 139 F. 366 (M.D.Pa. 1905).
[69] See *Depositors Trust Co. of August v. Frati Entertainment, Inc.*, 590 F.2d 377 (1st. Cir 1979).
[70] See 11 U.S.C. § 506(a)(1).
[71] See 11 U.S.C. § 553(a)(2); *In re U.S. Aeroteam, Inc.*, 327 B.R. 852 (S.D. Ohio 2005).
[72] See *In re Kittrell*, 23 C.B.C. 2d 1478 (Bankr.M.D.N.C. 1990).
[73] See 11 U.S.C. § 553(b).
[74] See 11 U.S.C. § 553(b).

Challenges To Secured Claims

Avoidance of Invalid or Unperfected Liens

A bankruptcy trustee can avoid invalid or unperfected liens.[75] The bankruptcy trustee has the same power to avoid a security interest as an unsecured creditor under state law.

Challenge to Extent of Value

In a case where the debtor is an individual, the value of collateral supporting a security interest is measured by its replacement value.[76] The Bankruptcy Code, however, is not nearly as clear on how to measure the value of collateral where the debtor is a business. Valuation can be a critical issue for creditors when determining if, or to what extent, their collateral's value is diminishing in the hands of the creditor. How, or to what extent the value of the collateral is diminishing, is a critical issue in determining what liens or cash payments are required to adequately protect a creditor. The debtor can argue that the value of the collateral is not decreasing significantly or is even increasing to minimize the measure of adequate protection to which a secured creditor is entitled. Similarly, the valuation of the collateral at the petition date can affect the extent of the secured creditor's interest in the collateral. To the extent that a court utilizes replacement, liquidation or going concern valuation approaches, the secured creditor's interest

---

[75] See 11 U.S.C. § 544; *In re Coleman*, 426 F.3d 710 (4th Cir. 2005).
[76] See 11 U.S.C. § 506; *American Commercial Corp. v. Rash*, 520 U.S. 953, 117 S.Ct. 1879 (1997).

in the collateral can be greatly affected.[77]

Another way in which valuation of collateral issues might arise is in a creditor's filing for relief from the automatic stay. One way for a creditor to be granted relief from the automatic stay is to show that the debtor has no equity in the collateral and that the property is not necessary to an effective reorganization.[78] To the extent that the creditor can show that the value of the lien on the property exceeds the fair market value of the property, and that the property is not necessary to an effective reorganization, the creditor will be granted relief from the automatic stay.[79]

Avoidance of Preferential Transfers

Transfers of security interests to a creditor are subject to avoidance actions. The creation of a security interest may be avoided if the creation or perfection of the security interest was to benefit a creditor for antecedent debt; made within ninety days of the petition date (one year in the case of insiders); and enabled the creditor to receive more than it would have received in a Chapter 7 liquidation if the transfer had not been made.[80]

Transfers to a fully secured creditor are generally not deemed preferential because a fully secured creditor is entitled to receive 100% of its claim even in a Chapter 7 liquidation.[81]

---

[77] See *U.S. v. Boccagna*, No. 04-5099-cr (2d. Cir. June 13, 2006).
[78] See 11 U.S.C. § 362(d).
[79] See 11 U.S.C. § 362(d).
[80] See 11 U.S.C. § 547.
[81] See *Triad International Maintenance v. SAT*, Case No. 2:04-cv-1200 (S.D.Ohio December 16 2005).

Avoidance of Fraudulent Transfers

The creation of a security interest is avoidable as a fraudulent transfer if the transfer was made within two years before the petition date and was made with the actual intent to hinder, delay or defraud. Similarly a security interest is avoidable as a fraudulent transfer if it was created within two years before the petition date with less than reasonably equivalent value in exchange when the debtor was Insolvent, at a time when the debtor was left with insufficient property for the operation of its business, or where the debtor intended to incur debts beyond its ability to repay.[82]

Challenge to Security Interest in Post-Petition Property of the Estate

Unless the pre-petition security agreement extends to the proceeds, offspring or profits of property existing pre-petition, property acquired by the estate or by the debtor after the commencement of the case is not subject to a secured party's lien that arose from a pre-petition security agreement.[83]

Equitable Subordination

The bankruptcy court has the authority to subordinate a claim on equitable grounds.[84] If a claimant engages in inequitable conduct that injures other creditors of the

---

[82] See 11 U.S.C. § 548.

[83] See 11 U.S.C. § 552; *In re Tower Air, Inc.*, 397 F.3d 191 (3d. Cir. 2005).

[84] See 11 U.S.C. § 510(c); *In re Enron*, 333 B.R. 205 (Bankr. S.D.N.Y. 2005).

estate, the bankruptcy court can subordinate that creditor's claim.[85]

Practical & Tactical

Balance sheets, valuations and evidence of consideration should be produced, understood and kept at the time any security interest is created and modified.

---

[85] See *In re Mobile Steel, Co.*, 563 F.2d 692 (1977).

CHAPTER 7
Issues Related to Vendors and Other Trade Creditors

Reclamation Claims

The Bankruptcy Code allows for reclamations.[86]   A creditor who ships goods to a debtor in the ordinary course of business may reclaim those goods if they were received while the debtor was insolvent and within forty-five days of the petition date, provided that the vendor makes written demand for the return of the goods before the earlier of: The end of 45 days from the date the goods were delivered to the debtor; or twenty days from

---

[86] See 11 U.S.C. § 546(c)(2).

the petition date.[87]

Consignment Claims

Goods shipped to the debtor on consignment are not property of the estate.[88] Caution should be used to ensure consignment agreements are properly documented.

Vendors who make timely reclamation claims, and consignors who have properly evidenced the consignment, are entitled to a return of their goods. Should the debtor desire to use these goods in its ongoing operations, the holder of the valid reclamation claim or consignment claim is entitled to timely payment of the full value of the goods it was entitled to recover.

> ## *Practical & Tactical*
> Vendors should track actual delivery dates (not shipping dates) for all goods shipped and promptly issue written *reclamation claims when they receive notice of a customer's bankruptcy.*
>
> Consignments should be carefully documented and processed to evidence the consignments and consignment return demands should be issued promptly upon notice of a consignee's bankruptcy. Uniform Commercial Code filings should be made in the appropriate filing office.

---

[87] See 11 U.S.C. § 546(c)(1); *In re Tucker*, 329 B.R. 291 (Bankr. D. Ariz. 2005).
[88] See *In re Altman*, 230 B.R. 6 (Bankr. Dacono. 1999).

Proofs of Claims

An unsecured creditor whose claim is either not listed on the debtor's schedules or is listed as disputed, contingent or unliquidated must file a proof of claim.[89] The bankruptcy court establishes deadlines for filing proofs of claim. If an unsecured creditor holding an otherwise allowable claim fails to timely file a proof of claim, the court will subordinate that creditor's claim to all timely filed claims.

---

[89] See 11 U.S.C. § 501

CHAPTER 8
Issues Related To Professionals

Chapter 11 reorganizations are complex and the debtor-in-possession will need a team of professional advisors. In most cases, the debtor will retain a law firm to act as lead bankruptcy counsel and an accounting firm to act as its accountants. In addition, the debtor may require the services of additional lawyers, investment bankers and other professionals to address its other needs during the reorganization. As a debtor-in-possession, the debtor generally cannot hire professionals without an order from the bankruptcy court.[90] Further, the professionals can only be paid with the approval of the bankruptcy court.[91]

[90] See 11 U.S.C. § 327.
[91] See 11 U.S.C. §§ 330 and 331.

Who May Be Employed

A debtor may, with the court's approval, employ attorneys, accountants, appraisers, auctioneers, agents, or other professionals that are necessary to the debtor's operation of its business.[92] Those professionals (attorneys, accountants, appraisers, auctioneers or other professionals) may only be retained to represent, or assist, a debtor-in-possession if they are disinterested.[93]

A person is disinterested if that person is not a creditor, equity security holder, or insider; was not an officer, director or employee of the debtor within two years before the petition date; and does not have an interest that is materially adverse to an interest of the estate or any class of creditors or equity holders.[94]

If the debtor-in-possession regularly employs attorneys, accountants or other professional persons on salary, the debtor may continue to so employ those professionals.[95]

A professional is not automatically disqualified from employment based on that professional's employment by, or representation of, a creditor in the case, unless there is an objection by another creditor or the United States Trustee. In the event of an objection by another creditor or the United States Trustee, the court will disallow the employment if there is an actual conflict of interest.[96]

---

[92] See 11 U.S.C. § 327.
[93] See 11 U.S.C. § 327.
[94] See 11 U.S.C. § 327(a).
[95] See 11 U.S.C. § 327(b).
[96] See 11 U.S.C. § 327(c).

Method of Employment

The bankruptcy court must approve the employment of any section 327(a) professionals retained by the debtor. In order to obtain approval by the bankruptcy court the debtor must submit an application to the court and the U.S. Trustee that outlines the employment and compensation to be paid for the services to be rendered.[97]

Misjudgments by professionals about what they must do when representing a debtor can have dire consequences. When I was a young attorney I was compelled to oppose the payment of a commission to a real estate agent who had undoubtedly done a great deal of work for a debtor, but was not entitled to a fee because of non-compliance with both section 327 and the local rules of the district in which the case was proceeding.

In another case, a very well respected firm serving as counsel to a Chapter 11 debtor-in-possession was deprived millions of dollars of fees it had otherwise earned in a major Chapter 11 reorganization because of its failure to fully disclose its representation of entities with claims against the debtor.

Applications for Compensation

Professionals employed by the debtor under section 327(a) may only be compensated as allowed by the court pursuant to sections 328-331.

A professional employed on behalf of the bankruptcy estate seeking compensation for services rendered or reimbursement for costs incurred must file an application for

---

[97] See 11 U.S.C. § 327, Fed. R. Bankr. Pro. 2014 and 2016.

compensation with the court along with a copy to the U.S. Trustee. The application for compensation must include a detailed account of the services rendered, time expended, expenses incurred and the amount requested.[98]

The court may award to a professional person reasonable compensation for actual, necessary services rendered by the professional; and reimbursement for actual, necessary expenses.[99]

The court may, in its own discretion or upon the motion of the United States Trustee or a party in interest, award less than the amount of compensation that is requested.[100] To determine what is reasonable compensation the court takes into account:

(A) the time spent on such services;

(B) the rate charged for such services;

(C) whether the services were necessary to the administration of, or beneficial at the time at which the service was rendered toward the completion of, a case under this title;

(D) whether the services were performed within a reasonable amount of time commensurate with the complexity, importance, and nature of the problem, issue, or task addressed;

(E) with respect to a professional person, whether the person is board certified or otherwise has demonstrated skill and experience in the bankruptcy field; and

(F) whether the compensation is reasonable based

---

[98] See Fed. R. Bankr. Pro. 2016.

[99] See 11 U.S.C. § 330(a)(1); *In re Patrick*, No. 04 B 38235 (Bankr.N.D.Ill. April 19 2006).

[100] See 11 U.S.C. § 330(a)(2); *In re Northwestern Corp.*, 05-396-JJF (D.Del. November 8 2005).

on the customary compensation charged by comparably skilled practitioners in cases other than cases under title 11.[101]

The bankruptcy court will not allow compensation for work it deems unnecessary or duplicative. Further, compensation will not be awarded for services that were not reasonably likely to benefit the estate or necessary to the administration of the case.[102]

Professionals employed under 327(a) are not required to wait to the end of the case for compensation. The Bankruptcy Code provides for the interim compensation of professionals employed under section 327(a). Those professionals employed under section 327(a) may apply to the court, during the case, for compensation for services rendered. The Bankruptcy Code permits professionals employed under section 327(a) to apply to the court not more than once every 120 days for interim compensation. However, the court may permit more frequent applications for interim compensation where the circumstances warrant a modification of this time constraint.[103]

Practical & Tactical

The importance of a proper conflict check to ensure disinterestedness cannot be overstated. In some cases, debtor's professionals have been compelled to waive entire fees billed in a Chapter 11 case because of a failure to identify and disclose a conflict.

---

[102] See 11 U.S.C. § 330(a)(3) and (4); *In re Garcia*, BAP No. SC-04-1591-NmoPa (9th Cir. December 7, 2005).
[103] See 11 U.S.C. § 331; *In re: PBA Tour Gear, Inc.*, 802-82195-dte, 82-82835-dte (Bankr.E.D.N.Y. July 5 2005).

CHAPTER 9
The Plan Of Reorganization

A debtor emerges from reorganization upon the confirmation of a plan of reorganization.

Who May File a Plan

A Chapter 11 debtor has the exclusive right to file a plan of reorganization for the first 120 days following the petition date.[104] If the debtor has not filed a plan within that 120 days, or does not succeed in having a plan confirmed within 180 days from the petition date, any creditor, equity security holder or indenture trustee may

---

[104] See 11 U.S.C. § 1§ 1121; *In re Burns and Roe Enterprises, Inc.*, Case No. 00-41610 RG (D.N.J. November 2 2005).

file a Plan. Upon a showing of cause, the court may extend either period.

Disclosure and Solicitation

In Chapter 11 cases (other than small business cases as defined under section 101(51C)), the proponent of a plan of reorganization must obtain approval of its disclosure statement before it can distribute the plan and disclosure statement to solicit votes. To obtain approval of the disclosure statement, the proponent must demonstrate that the disclosure statement contains adequate information to allow the holder of a claim (or interest) to make an informed decision about whether to vote for or against the plan of reorganization.[105]

Classification

Generally, claims and interests must be classified with other claims and interests that are substantially similar. However, the plan may separate out a class of unsecured claims that are less than, or reduced to, a certain amount for administrative convenience. [106]

The bankruptcy code prescribes what must be Included, and what may be included in a Chapter 11 plan of reorganization.[107]   The plan must designate classes of creditors. Generally, plans classify each secured claim in

---

[105] See 11 U.S.C. § 1§ 1125; *In re FiberMARK, Inc.*, Case No. 04-10463 (Bankr. D.Vt. December 2, 2005).
[106] See 11 U.S.C. 1122; *In re Enron Corp.*, Case No. 01-16034 (AJG)(Bankr. S.D.N.Y. July 15 2004).
[107] See 11 U.S.C. § 1§ 1123; *In re New Power Co.*, 438 F.3d 1113 (11th Cir. 2006).

a separate class, classify priority unsecured claims in classes of similar priority claims and combine general unsecured creditors into one class. Other classes may also include a convenience class and a class of equity security holders.

The plan must treat similar claims in a similar manner.

Impairment of Classes

Under the code, the plan may impair classes of creditors.[108] An impaired class is a class of claims that will not receive full payment or that will have some legal, contractual or equitable right altered. If under the plan certain classes are impaired, the plan must specify which classes are impaired, and how those impaired classes will be treated. If a debtor's plan impairs any class of creditors, the plan will not be confirmed without the approval of at least one impaired class.[109]

Cram Down

It is possible for a plan of reorganization to be confirmed over the objections of dissenting creditors or impaired classes of creditors. This method of confirmation is referred to as "cram down." If all of the requirements for plan confirmation have been met, except that an impaired class has objected to confirmation, the court may approve the plan so long as the court finds that the plan is fair and equitable to each impaired class and

---

[108] See 11 U.S.C. §§ 1§ 1123, 1124; *In re G.L. Bryan Investments, Inc.*, 04-21867-SBB (Bankr.D.Colo. March 8 2006).
[109] See 11 U.S.C. § 1§ 1126; *In re Armstrong World Industries, Inc.*, 432 F.3d 507 (3d Cir. 2005).

does not unfairly discriminate against a specific class.

Confirmation

Voting and Acceptance

A plan is accepted by a class of claims if claimants who are at least one-half of the creditors holding allowed claims and hold at least two thirds of the dollar amount of the allowed claims vote to accept the plan.[110] If either less than half the holders of claims or less than two thirds of the dollar amount of the allowed claims in a class vote to accept a plan, the class is deemed to have not accepted the plan.

Hearing on Confirmation

After notice, the court must hold a confirmation hearing at which a party in interest may object to the confirmation of the bankruptcy plan.[111]

General Requirements

In order to confirm a Chapter 11 plan of reorganization, the bankruptcy court must find that all relevant requirements have been satisfied. The plan must

---

[110] See 11 U.S.C. § 1§ 1129; *In re Armstrong World Industries, Inc.*, 432 F.3d 507 (3d Cir. 2005).
[111] See 11 U.S.C. § 1§ 1128; *In re Scott Cable Communications, Inc.*, Bankr. No. 98-51923 (AHWS) Bankr. Adversary No. 98CV5104(AWT) (Dacono. March 12 2001).

conform to the requirements of Section 1123. All administrative claims must be paid in full or on such terms as the holder of those claims agrees to accept. No distribution can be made to a subordinate class unless the prior class has been paid in full, or on such terms as that class has agreed to accept. Before votes for a plan were solicited, the debtor must have had its disclosure statement approved by the court (unless the solicitation occurred pre-petition in the course of proposing a pre-packaged Chapter 11).

Confirmation of the debtor's Chapter 11 plan allows the debtor to emerge from the reorganization process. Confirmation of the plan binds the debtor to the provisions of the plan, vests property of the bankruptcy estate with the debtor and discharges the debtor from any debt that arose before the date of the bankruptcy petition (except as provided for under the plan or order confirming the plan).[112]

A creditor whose interest will be impaired by a plan has two distinct rights with regard to a proposed plan of reorganization. One is the right to vote for or against confirmation (the creditor may vote its claim based upon nothing more than its own business interests as it perceives those interests). The other is the right to object to the plan or disclosure statement to the extent that the creditor believes that they do not satisfy the requirements of the Bankruptcy Code.

On numerous occasions our firm, as counsel for various creditors, has had to respond to plans that were unfavorable to our clients. In my experience, a well

---

[112] See 11 U.S.C. § 1§ 1141; *In re Friedberg*, 192 B.R. 338 (S.D.N.Y. 1996); *In re Frank's Nursery & Crafts, Inc.*, Case No. 04-15826 (PCB) (Bankr. S.D.N.Y. May 18, 2006).

drafted objection to a disclosure statement and/or plan of reorganization can be of great assistance in helping the debtor's attorney understand why a creditor's claim should either be reclassified within a plan or afforded different treatment than originally proposed. Of course, the question of whether certain claims are so substantially similar that they should be classified together as a class is often subjective and there is often room for qualified counsel to influence counsel for the plan proponent and/or the court.

For example, when representing major forestry product and land development companies in the reorganization of a manufacturer of a water management system that was believed to have a major design defect, we argued that although the design defect had not yet manifested itself with a total product failure at our clients' installations, none-the-less our clients' claims should be treated the same as the claims of purchasers whose products had manifested the product design defect through a total system failure. The holders of claims for products that had evidenced the design defects with a complete system collapse wanted their claims paid, but did not want payment to creditors whose systems had not yet failed -- claiming that if they had not yet failed, they were not defective. It may have been because our client could have objected to the classification of its claim, the adequacy of the disclosure statement and the confirmation of the plan that the debtor agreed that our client had an allowed claim for a defective product. In the context of this case, the debtor agreed that the mere fact that certain installation factors had delayed the ultimate system failure did not mean that there was not a design defect for which our client had a valid claim. Absent a solid understanding of its Chapter 11 rights, these companies would have had a much more difficult product liability case given the fact that their particular system had not yet manifested its failure.

The plan of reorganization may be confirmed if it complies with the requirements of the Bankruptcy Code, was proposed in good faith and was voted for by at least the majority in number and two thirds the amount of at least one impaired class.[113]

An order confirming a plan must find that:

- The plan complies with the applicable provisions of Chapter 11 of the Code;
- The debtor complies with the applicable provisions of the Code;
- The plan has been proposed in good faith;
- Any payment made or promised by the debtor has been disclosed to the court and that payment was reasonable;
- The debtor has disclosed the identity of any insider that will be employed or retained by the reorganized debtor, and the nature of the compensation to the insider;
- No regulatory commission has jurisdiction over the rates of the debtor;
- With respect to each class of claims, each class has accepted the plan or is not impaired under the plan (which is defined herein as not receiving an amount less than the amount it would have received had the debtor liquidated under Chapter 7);
- Confirmation of the plan is not likely to be followed by the liquidation, or the need for further financial reorganization of the debtor or any successor; and

---

[113] See 11 U.S.C. 1129.

- Parties were provided with adequate notice of the deadline to object to discharge.

Types of Plans

Earnouts

An Earnout is a form of Chapter 11 plan of reorganization in which the debtor's net earnings are expected to pay a dividend to holders of allowed pre-petition claims.

Going Concern Sales

A Chapter 11 plan of reorganization funded by the sale of the debtor's business as a going concern is a common exit strategy for a debtor-in-possession. Boiled down to its most simple components, the debtor sells its business as a going concern and the proceeds of the sale are distributed among its creditors in accordance with the requirements of Section 1129.

Asset Sales

A debtor may also exit with a Chapter 11 plan of reorganization funded by the liquidation of its assets without the continued operation of the business. The assets are usually sold at an auction to multiple buyers or in a negotiated transaction to one or more buyers after notice to the creditors and other parties in interest, subject to higher and better offers.

Combinations

A Chapter 11 plan may involve a combination of an earnout, a going concern sale and/or an asset sale.

Pre-Packs

A pre-pack is a Chapter 11 plan of reorganization that is negotiated before the case is filed so that the process, from filing to confirmation, is faster and more cost efficient.   A pre-pack may be in any of the forms discussed above.

CHAPTER 10
Other Considerations

Chapter 11 reorganizations are complex, stressful for debtor's management and can be very expensive. However, the potential rewards from a well managed interest in a Chapter 11 reorganization can produce outstanding results.

A successful Chapter 11 reorganization may increase a creditor's return by large margins. The difference between what creditors would get without a reorganization and what they can expect to recover from a successful reorganization will often represent a return on investment that will exceed the return on most other investments.

Ethical Considerations

In the context of a Chapter 11 reorganization, the conduct of many of the participants will be constrained by ethical considerations. Without an understanding of these ethical constraints, professionals and their clients can be exposed to dire consequences. With a proper understanding of these ethical constraints, one can better understand the actions of the other parties to a case and what options are available to maximize the return on investment.

The Debtor

The debtor, its management and counsel owe a fiduciary duty to the entire bankruptcy estate and its creditors in a Chapter 11 reorganization. The debtor is charged with attempting to maximize the recovery of all creditors with allowed claims in accordance with the priorities established by the United States Bankruptcy Code. A corollary to that obligation is the obligation to seek the disallowance of those claims that are not properly allowable against the estate.

The debtor's management is ethically prohibited from engaging in self-dealing.

A common ethical problem for management arises when there are possible claims against the debtor's insiders that should be the basis for an adversary proceeding against those insiders (such as an action to avoid a preferential transfer).

The Creditors' Committee

The official committee of unsecured creditors, and its counsel, are charged with seeking to maximize the recovery for the holders of allowed unsecured claims.

The members of the creditors' committee and their attorneys owe a fiduciary duty to the class of general unsecured creditors.[114] Members of the creditors' committee cannot use their position on that committee for their own personal gain.

In some cases, a creditors' committee can be faced with a conflict within the class of general unsecured creditors that can only be resolved by the formation of another committee with separate counsel.

To resolve a conflict of this nature, the creditors' committee should support the formation of a new committee to represent this separate group.

---

[114] *In re Refco*, 336 B.R. 187, 195 (Bankr. S.D.N.Y. 2006).

CHAPTER 11
Conclusion

Bankruptcy is a complex and exciting area of the law. The Bankruptcy Code and the decisions interpreting it are rational and make sense - once you see how they fit together. There are a myriad of opportunities within the bankruptcy process to reduce losses, acquire key assets and earn outstanding results for those business leaders who understand how this process works.

It is my belief that with the proper tools to understand Chapter 11 business reorganizations, business leaders can evaluate the options for the deployment of assets within business reorganizations to realize superior return on investment. I also believe that with the appropriate information, accountants and general counsel can

better serve their business clients by helping them spot potential problems and opportunities.

In writing this book, it was my hope to remove much of the mystery of Chapter 11 business reorganizations and share some practical and tactical advice gleaned from twenty years of practice in this field.   By reading this book and using its glossary and selected sections from the Bankruptcy Code, I hope that you will find it easier to understand both the problems and the opportunities that are common in Chapter 11 business reorganizations.

GLOSSARY

Unless otherwise indicated, all section references are to section of the United States Bankruptcy Code, 11 U.S.C. § 101, et. Seq.

Accountant: A certified public accountant, professional association, corporation or partnership authorized to provide certified public accounting.

Actual Fraud: Fraud conducted with the actual intent to hinder, delay or defraud a creditor.

Administrative Claim: A claim for goods or services actually provided to the debtor post-petition is entitled to priority over most pre-petition claims. See § 503.

Administrative Claimant: The holder of an administrative claim.

Administrative Expense: The actual, necessary costs and expenses of preserving the bankruptcy estate. See § 503(b)(1)(A).

Adequate Assurance: Sufficient guarantee of performance of terms of an Executory contract to permit a debtor to assume an executory contract after there has been a default. See § 365(b).

Adequate Protection: Cash payments, new security interests in additional collateral or other relief to replace a diminution in the value of a party's secured party's interest in its collateral with the indubitable equivalent of such party's interest. See § 361.

Adversary Proceeding: A lawsuit filed in bankruptcy court that is related to the debtor's bankruptcy case. Bankruptcy Rule 7001.

Affiliate: (1) An entity that owns, controls, or holds with the power to vote, 20 percent or more of the outstanding voting securities of the debtor; (2) A corporation where 20 percent or more of whose outstanding voting securities are owned or indirectly owned, controlled or held with the power to vote, by the debtor, or by the entity that directly or indirectly owns, controls , or holds with power to vote, 20 percent or more of the outstanding voting securities of the debtor; (3) A person whose business is operated under a lease or operating agreement by the debtor, or person substantially all of whose property is operated under an operating agreement of the debtor; or (4) An entity that operates the business or substantially all the property of the debtor under a lease or operating agreement. 11 U.S.C. 101(3).

Allowed Claim: A claim against the debtor that has

either been deemed allowed, or was allowed after a hearing. See § 502.

Attorney: An attorney at law, professional law association, corporation, or partnership authorized to practice law.

Assignment: The process by which the debtor transfers an assumed executory contract to another party. See § 365(f).

Assumption: The process by which the debtor reaffirms an executory contract. See § 365.

Automatic Stay: An injunction automatically issued by the bankruptcy court when a debtor files for bankruptcy that prohibits most creditor collection activities such as filing or continuing lawsuits, making written requests for payment, or notifying creditor reporting bureaus of an unpaid debt. See § 362.

Avoidance Powers: The right and power of the Bankruptcy Trustee to undo certain transfers made by the debtor and certain obligations incurred by the debtor. See § 544.

Bankruptcy Estate: All legal or equitable interests of the debtor in property as of the commencement of the case. See § 541(a)(1).

Bankruptcy Trustee: The representative of the bankruptcy estate. See § 323.

Bona Fide Dispute: A dispute that is genuine, interposed for legitimate purposes, and not merely contrived for strategic advantage. See § 303.

Bona Fide Purchaser: A purchaser who purchases for fair consideration in good faith. See §§ 547, 548.

Buyer in Ordinary Course of Business: A party buys goods in the ordinary course if the sale to the person comports with the usual or customary practices in the kind of business in which the seller is engaged or with the seller's own usual or customary practices. Uniform Commercial Code § 1-201(b)(9).

Cash Collateral: Cash and cash equivalents in which the debtor has an interest that is subject to the security interest of a creditor of the debtor. See § 363(a).

Claim: Right to payment, or equitable remedy, regardless of whether that right is unliquidated, contingent or unmatured. See § 101(5).

Collateral: Property subject to a security interest. U.C.C. 9-102(a)(12).

Confirmation: Bankruptcy court's approval of the plan of reorganization in a Chapter 11 case. See § 1129.

Corporation: A corporation includes: (1) an association having a power or privilege that a private corporation possesses; (2) a partnership association organized under a law that makes only the capital subscribed responsible for the debts of such association; (3) a joint-stock company; (4) an unincorporated business; and (5) a business trust. A corporation does not include a limited partnership. 11 U.S.C. 101(9).

Creditor: The holder of claim that arose before the debtor filed its petition.

Creditors' Committee: Generally used to refer to the

official committee appointed by the United States Trustee to represent the interests of the allowed general unsecured creditors. See § 1102.

Custodian: A receiver or trustee of property of the debtor. See § 543 and § 101(11).

Debt: A debt is liability on a claim. See § 101(12)

Debtor: A person or municipality for whom, or under which, a bankruptcy case under Title 11 has been commenced. See § 101(13).

Debtor-In-Possession: The debtor in a Chapter 11 case in which no trustee has been appointed. 11 U.S.C. 1101(1).

D-I-P Financing: A debtor's post-petition borrowing of money, usually on a secured basis. See § 364.

Disclosure Statement: A document describing a plan of reorganization in a manner calculated to provide the necessary information for claimants to make an informed decision about whether to vote for or against confirmation of plan.

Discharge: The release of the debtor from liability for certain dischargeable debts that prevent the creditors owed those debts from taking any action against the debtor to collect those debts. See § 524.

Disinterested Person: A person that is not: a creditor, equity security holder, an insider, an investment banker for any outstanding security of the debtor, an investment banker for a security of the debtor within the past three years, an officer/director/employee of the debtor within the past two years, or a person with a materially adverse interest of the estate or a class of creditors. See § 101(14).

Entity: Persons, estate, trust, governmental unit, and the United States Trustee. See § 101(15).

Equity: The value of the debtor's interest in property.

Equity Cushion: The amount by which the fair market value of collateral exceed the claim(s) secured by that collateral. See § 506(b).

Equity Security: (1) share in a corporation; (2) interest of a limited partner; or (3) warrant or right, other than a right to convert, to purchase, sell or subscribe to a share, security, or interest in either a share in a corporation or interest of a limited partner. See § 101(16).

Estate: That which is created by the commencement of a case under The United States Bankruptcy Code and contains all the property in which the debtor has a legal or equitable interest as more fully defined in § 541.

Equity Security Holder: The holder of an equity security of the debtor. See § 101(17).

Examiner: A person appointed to investigate a debtor. The examiner does not replace a debtor-in-possession the way that a trustee does. See § 1104.

Executory Contract: A contract where there is something left to be done by both of the parties to the transaction. See § 365.

Fiduciary Duty: The duty of utmost care and loyalty to the interest of another. A debtor has a fiduciary duty to protect the estate and the interests of creditors. A creditors' committee has fiduciary duty to all holders of allowed general unsecured creditors. See § 1102.

Financial Institution: A federal reserve bank, commercial bank, savings bank, industrial savings bank, savings and loan association, trust company, federally insured credit Union, etc. See § 101(22).

Franchise: A grant of authority, often including licenses to the franchisee that permits the franchisee to sell or otherwise use products and/or services of the franchisor.

Franchisor: An entity that grants to others the license to operate one of its franchises.

Franchisee: An entity that is granted the license to operate a franchise by a franchisor.

Fraudulent Transfer: The transfer of property where either the debtor has the actual intent to defraud creditors or where the debtor receives less than a reasonably equivalent value for the transfer. See § 548.

General Unsecured Claim: A pre-petition obligation of the debtor that is not entitled to priority and is not secured by collateral that is property of the debtor. See § 507.

Good faith: Observance of reasonable commercial standards of fair dealing. U.C.C. 1-201(b)(20).

Governmental Unit: The United States, any state, commonwealth, district, territory, municipality, foreign state, department, agency, or instrumentality of the United States, or any other foreign or domestic government. See § 101(27).

Indenture: A mortgage, deed of trust, or indenture, under which there is outstanding a security constituting a claim against the debtor, a claim secured by a lien on any of the debtor's property, or an equity security of the debtor. See § 101(28).

Indenture Trustee: A trustee under an indenture. 11 U.S.C. 101(29).

Insider: An insider includes:
A. If the debtor is an <u>individual:</u>
1. Relative or general partner of the individual;
2. Partnership in which the debtor is a general partner;
3. Corporation of which the debtor is a director, officer or person in control;
B. If the debtor is a <u>corporation:</u>
1. Director of the debtor;
2. Officer of the debtor;
3. Person in control of the debtor;
4. Partnership in which the debtor is a general partner;
5. General partner of the debtor;
6. Relative of a general partner, director, officer, or person in control of the debtor;
C. If the debtor is a Partnership-
1. General partner in the debtor;
2. Relative of a general partner in, general partner of, or person in control of the debtor;
3. Partnership in which the debtor is a general partner;
4. General partner of the debtor; or
5. Person in control of the debtor. See § 101(31).

Insolvent: (a) having generally ceased to pay debts in the ordinary course of business other than as a result of a bona fide dispute; (b) being unable to pay debts as they become due; or (c) being insolvent within the meaning of federal bankruptcy law. U.C.C. 1-201(b)(23).

Insolvent (within the meaning of federal bankruptcy law): The sum of the entity's debts is greater than all of the entity's property, at fair valuation (exclusive of property transferred, concealed or removed with the intent to hinder or delay creditors and property that may be exempt from property of the estate). See § 101(32)(A).

Intellectual Property: Trade secrets, patents, copyrights, trademarks, and mask work to the extent protected by non-bankruptcy law. See § 101(35A).

Inventory: Goods, other than farm products which: are leased; are held for sale or lease; are furnished by a person under a contract of service; or consist of raw materials, work in progress or materials used or consumed in business. U.C.C. 9-102(a)(48).

Ipso Facto Clause: A clause in a contract that provides that the contract will terminate automatically upon the debtor's filing for protection from creditors under the United States Bankruptcy Code. A clause that is unenforceable as against public policy. See § 365(e)(1).

Judicial Lien: A lien obtained by judgment, levy or sequestration, or other legal or equitable process. See § 101(36).

Lien: A charge against or interest in property to secure payment of a debt or performance of an obligation. See § 101(37).

Nondischargeable Debt: A debt that cannot be eliminated in bankruptcy. See § 523.

Order for Relief: Commencement of a voluntary bankruptcy case. See § 301.

Person: An individual, partnership, limited liability company, or corporation. A person, generally, does not include a governmental unit. See § 101(41).

Petition: A document filed pursuant to sections 301, 302, 303 or 304 in bankruptcy court commencing a bankruptcy case.

Petition Date: The date on which the petition for relief from creditors is filed with the bankruptcy court.

Plan of Reorganization: The arrangement proposed by the debtor, or its creditors after the exclusive period, which if approved by the court restructures the debtor's obligations to its creditors. See Sections 1122, 1123 and 1129.

Post-Petition: Arising after the petition date.

Preferential Transfer: A transfer of property, or the creation of an obligation, made by the debtor within 90 days before the filing petition date, or one year in the case of insiders. See § 547(b).

Pre-Petition: Arising before the petition date.

Priority: Ranking of unsecured claims to determine the order of payment. See § 507;

Proof of Claim: The document filed by a creditor asserting that creditor's claim. See § 501.

Proof of Interest: The document filed by an equity security holder asserting that party's equity interest. See § 501.

Pro Rata Share: The share or amount to be received by an individual that is in proportion to the amount or share to be received by others with a similar entitlement. See § 507.

Purchaser: The transferee of a voluntary transfer, and includes immediate or mediate transferee of such a transferee. See § 101(43).

Rejection: A debtor's election to terminate an executory contract. See § 365.

Relative: An individual related by marriage or blood within the third degree as determined by the common law, or an individual in a step or adoptive relationship within the third degree. See § 101(45).

Relief from Automatic Stay: An order from the court allowing a party to continue/commence an action that was stopped/prohibited by the filing automatic stay. See § 362(d).

Safe Harbor: A section of a statute that defines conditions under which a party is protected from the application of laws that might otherwise render permitted action impermissible. See § 547(c).

Section 341 Meeting: The meeting of the creditors, scheduled by the U.S. Trustee. See § 341(a).

Secured Creditor: A creditor that holds a validly perfected security interest in property of the estate for at least a portion of its claim. See § 506.

Security: A security includes: note, stock, treasury stock, bond, debenture, collateral trust certificate, pre-organization certificate or subscription, transferable share, voting-trust certificate, certificate of deposit, certificate of deposit for security, investment contract, interest of a limited partner, and certificate of interest in a security. A security does not include: currency, check, bill, draft, bank letter of credit, leverage transaction, commodity futures contract or forward contract, an option to purchase or sell a commodity futures contract, an option to sell a commodity or debt. See § 101(49).

Security Agreement: An agreement that creates or provides for a security interest. See § 101(50).

Security Interest: An interest in personal property or fixtures that secures payment or performance of an obligation. U.C.C. 1-201(b)(35).

Set-Off: A creditor's claim against the debtor that it is entitled to reduce the amount of the debt it owes the debtor because of a mutual debt owed by the debtor to the creditor. See § 553.

Small Business Case: A case filed under Chapter 11 in which the debtor is a small business debtor. See § 101(51C).

Small Business Debtor: A debtor engaged in commercial or business activities that has aggregate non-contingent liquidated secured and unsecured debt of $2,000,000 or less for which no creditors' committee has been appointed. See § 101 (51D).

Statutory Lien: Lien arising solely by force of a statute on specified circumstances or conditions. See § 101(53).

Surety: A guarantor or other secondary obligor. U.C.C. 1-201(b)(39).

Transfer: Creation of a lien, foreclosure of the debtor's right of redemption or each mode, direct or indirect, absolute or conditional, voluntary or involuntary, of disposing of, or parting with, property or an interest in property. See § 101(54).

Trustee: In the context of a Chapter 11, a person appointed by the court upon a finding of cause - Such as fraud, dishonesty or incompetence by the debtor. See § 1104.

UCC: The Uniform Commercial Code. The UCC is adopted on a state-by-state basis.

UFTA: The Uniform Fraudulent Transfer Act. The UFTA is adopted on a state-by-state basis.

US Trustee: The United States Trustee program is a component of the Department of Justice that seeks to promote the efficiency and protect the integrity of the Federal bankruptcy system. To further the public interest in the just, speedy and economical resolution of cases filed under the Bankruptcy Code, the program monitors the conduct of bankruptcy parties and private estate trustees, oversees related administrative functions, and acts to ensure compliance with applicable laws and procedures. It also identifies and helps investigate bankruptcy fraud and abuse in coordination with United States Attorneys, the Federal Bureau of Investigation, and other law enforcement agencies.

Voluntary Petition: The document filed by a debtor to commence its own bankruptcy case.

U.S. Bankruptcy Code
Selected Sections

§ 109 Who may be a debtor

(a) Notwithstanding any other provision of this section, only a person that resides or has a domicile, a place of business, or property in the United States, or a municipality, may be a debtor under this title. . . .

§ 301 Voluntary Cases

(a) A voluntary case under a chapter of this title is commenced by the filing with the Bankruptcy Court of a petition under such chapter by an entity that may be a debtor under such chapter.

(b) The commencement of a voluntary case under a chapter of this title constitutes an order for relief under such chapter.

§ 303 Involuntary Cases

(a) An involuntary case may be commenced only under chapter 7 or 11 of this title, and only against a person, except a farmer, family farmer, or a corporation that is not a moneyed, business, or commercial corporation, that may be a debtor under the chapter under which such case is commenced.

(b) An involuntary case against a person is commenced by the filing with the Bankruptcy Court of a petition under chapter 7 or 11 of this title—

(1) by three or more entities, each of which is either a holder of a claim against such person that is not contingent as to liability or the subject of a bona fide dispute, as to liability or among or an indenture trustee representing such a holder, if such noncontingent, undisputed claims aggregate at least $10,000 more than the value of any lien on property of the debtor securing such claims held by the holders of such claims;

(2) if there are fewer than 12 such holders, excluding any employee or insider of such person and any transferee of a transfer that is voidable under section 544, 545, 547, 548, 549, or 724 (a) of this title, by one or more of such holders that hold in the aggregate at least $10,000 of such claims;

(3) if such person is a partnership—

(A) by fewer than all of the general partners in such partnership; or

(B) if relief has been ordered under this title with respect to all of the general partners in such partnership, by a general partner in such partnership, the trustee of such a general partner, or a holder of a claim against such partnership; or

(4) by a foreign representative of the estate in a foreign proceeding concerning such person.

(c) After the filing of a petition under this section but before the case is dismissed or relief is ordered, a creditor holding an unsecured claim that is not contingent, other than a creditor filing under subsection (b) of this section, may join in the petition with the same effect as if such joining creditor were a petitioning creditor under subsection (b) of this section.

(d) The debtor, or a general partner in a partnership debtor that did not join in the petition, may file an answer to a petition under this section.

(e) After notice and a hearing, and for cause, the court may require the petitioners under this section to file a bond to indemnify the debtor for such amounts as the court may later allow under subsection (i) of this section.

(f) Notwithstanding section 363 of this title, except to the extent that the court orders otherwise, and until an order for relief in the case, any business of the debtor may continue to operate, and the debtor may continue to use, acquire, or dispose of property as if an involuntary case concerning the debtor had not been commenced.

(g) At any time after the commencement of an involuntary case under chapter 7 of this title but before an order for relief in the case, the court, on request of a party in interest, after notice to the debtor and a hearing, and if necessary to preserve the property of the estate or to prevent loss to the estate, may order the United States trustee to appoint an interim trustee under section 701 of this title to take possession of the property of the estate and to operate any business of the debtor. Before an order for relief, the debtor may regain possession of property in the possession of a trustee ordered appointed under this subsection if the debtor files such bond as the court requires, conditioned on the debtor's accounting for and delivering to the trustee, if there is an order for relief in the case, such property, or the value, as of the date the debtor regains possession, of such property.

(h) If the petition is not timely controverter, the court shall order relief against the debtor in an involuntary case under the chapter under which the petition was filed. Otherwise, after trial, the court shall order relief against the debtor in an involuntary case under the chapter under which the petition was filed, only if—

(1) the debtor is generally not paying such debtor's debts as such debts become due unless such debts are the subject of a bona fide dispute as to liability or amount; or

(2) within 120 days before the date of the filing of the petition, a custodian, other than a trustee, receiver, or agent appointed or authorized to take charge of less than substantially all of the property of the debtor for the purpose of enforcing a lien against such property, was appointed or took possession.

(i) the court dismisses a petition under this section other than on consent of all petitioners and the debtor, and if the debtor does not waive the right to judgment under this subsection, the court may grant judgment—

(1) against the petitioners and in favor of the debtor for—

(A) costs; or

(B) a reasonable attorney's fee; or

(2) against any petitioner that filed the petition in bad faith, for—

(A) any damages proximately caused by such filing; or

(B) punitive damages.

(j) Only after notice to all creditors and a hearing may the court dismiss a petition filed under this section—

(1) on the motion of a petitioner;

(2) on consent of all petitioners and the debtor; or

(3) for want of prosecution.

(k) Repealed.   Pub. L. 109-8, title VIII, Sec. 802(d)(2), Apr. 20, 2005,

119 Stat. 146

(I)

(1) If —

(A) the petition under this section is false or contains any materially false, fictitious, or fraudulent statement;

(B) the debtor is an individual; and

(C) the court dismisses such petition, the court, upon the motion of the debtor, shall seal all the records of the court relating to such petition, and all references to such petition.

(2) If the debtor is an individual and the court dismisses a petition under this section, the court may enter an order prohibiting all consumer reporting agencies (as defined in section 603(f) of the Fair Credit Reporting Act (15 U.S.C. 1681a(f))) from making any consumer report (as defined in section 603(d) of that Act) that contains any information relating to such petition or to the case commenced by the filing of such petition.

(3) Upon the expiration of the statute of limitations described in section 3282 of title 18, for a violation of section 152 or 157 of such title, the court, upon the motion of the debtor and for good cause, may expunge any records relating to a petition filed under this section.

§ 323 Role and Capacity of trustee

(a) The trustee in a case under this title is the representative of the estate.

(b) The trustee in a case under this title has capacity to sue and be sued.

§ 327 Employment of professional persons

(a) Except as otherwise provided in this section, the trustee, with the court's approval, may employ one or more attorneys, accountants, appraisers, auctioneers, or other professional persons, that do not hold or represent an interest adverse to the estate, and that are disinterested persons, to represent or assist the trustee in carrying out the trustee's duties under this title.

(b) If the trustee is authorized to operate the business of the debtor under section 721, 1202, or 1108 of this title, and if the debtor has regularly employed attorneys, accountants, or other professional persons on salary, the trustee may retain or replace such professional persons if necessary in the operation of such business.

(c) In a case under chapter 7, 12, or 11 of this title, a person is not disqualified for employment under this section solely because of such person's employment by or representation of a creditor, unless there is objection by another creditor or the United States trustee, in which case the court shall disapprove such employment if there is an actual conflict of interest.

(d) The court may authorize the trustee to act as attorney or accountant for the estate if such authorization is in the best interest of the estate.

(e) The trustee, with the court's approval, may employ, for a specified special purpose, other than to represent the trustee in conducting the case, an attorney that has represented the debtor, if in the best interest of the estate, and if such attorney does not represent or hold any interest adverse to the debtor or to the estate with respect to the matter on which such attorney is to be employed.

(f) The trustee may not employ a person that has served as an examiner in the case.

§ 330 Compensation of officers

(a)

(1) After notice to the parties in interest and the United States Trustee and a hearing, and subject to sections 326, 328, and 329, the court may award to a trustee, a consumer privacy ombudsman appointed under section 332, an examiner, an ombudsman appointed under section 333, or a professional person employed under section 327 or 1103—

(A) reasonable compensation for actual, necessary services rendered by the trustee, examiner, ombudsman, professional person, or attorney and by any paraprofessional person employed by any such person; and

(B) reimbursement for actual, necessary expenses.

(2) The court may, on its own motion or on the motion of the United States Trustee, the United States Trustee for the District or Region, the trustee for the estate, or any other party in interest, award compensation that is less than the amount of compensation that is requested.

(3) In determining the amount of reasonable compensation to be awarded to an examiner, trustee under Chapter 11, or professional person, the court shall consider the nature, the extent, and the value of such services, taking into account all relevant factors, including—

(A) the time spent on such services;

(B) the rates charged for such services;

(C) whether the services were necessary to the administration of, or beneficial at the time at which the service was rendered toward the completion of, a case under this title;

(D) whether the services were performed within a reasonable amount of time commensurate with the complexity, importance, and nature of the problem, issue, or task addressed;

(E) with respect to a professional person, whether the person is board certified or otherwise has demonstrated skill and experience in the bankruptcy field; and

(F) whether the compensation is reasonable based on the

customary compensation charged by comparably skilled practitioners in cases other than cases under this title.

(4)

(A) Except as provided in subparagraph (B), the court shall not allow compensation for—

(i) unnecessary duplication of services; or

(ii) services that were not—

(I) reasonably likely to benefit the debtor's estate; or

(II) necessary to the administration of the case.

(B) In a chapter 12 or chapter 13 case in which the debtor is an individual, the court may allow reasonable compensation to the debtor's attorney for representing the interests of the debtor in connection with the bankruptcy case based on a consideration of the benefit and necessity of such services to the debtor and the other factors set forth in this section.

(5) The court shall reduce the amount of compensation awarded under this section by the amount of any interim compensation awarded under section 331, and, if the amount of such interim compensation exceeds the amount of compensation awarded under this section, may order the return of the excess to the estate.

(6) Any compensation awarded for the preparation of a fee application shall be based on the level and skill reasonably required to prepare the application.

(7) In determining the amount of reasonable compensation to be awarded to a trustee, the court shall treat such compensation as commission, based on section 326.

(b)

(1) There shall be paid from the filing fee in a case under chapter 7 of this title $45 to the trustee serving in such case, after such trustee's services are rendered.

(2) The Judicial Conference of the United States—

(A) shall prescribe additional fees of the same kind as prescribed under section 1914 (b) of title 28; and

(B) may prescribe notice of appearance fees and fees charged against distributions in cases under this title; to pay $15 to trustees serving in cases after such trustees' services are rendered. Beginning 1 year after the date of the enactment of the Bankruptcy Reform Act of 1994, such $15 shall be paid in addition to the amount paid under paragraph (1).

(c) Unless the court orders otherwise, in a case under chapter 12 or 13 of this title the compensation paid to the trustee serving in the case shall not be less than $5 per month from any distribution under the plan during the administration of the plan.

(d) In a case in which the United States trustee serves as trustee, the compensation of the trustee under this section shall be paid to the clerk of the Bankruptcy Court and deposited by the clerk into the United States Trustee System Fund established by section 589a of title 28.

§ 341 Meeting of creditors and equity security holders

(a) Within a reasonable time after the order for relief in a case under this title, the United States trustee shall convene and preside at a meeting of creditors.

(b) The United States trustee may convene a meeting of any equity security holders.

(c) The court may not preside at, and may not attend, any meeting under this section including any final meeting of creditors. Notwithstanding any local court rule, provision of a State constitution, any otherwise applicable nonbankruptcy law, or any other requirement that representation at the meeting of creditors under subsection (a) be by an attorney, a creditor holding a consumer debt or any representative of the creditor (which may include an entity or an employee of an entity and may be a representative for more than 1 creditor) shall be permitted to appear at and participate in the meeting of creditors in a case under chapter 7 or 13, either alone or in conjunction with an attorney for the creditor. Nothing in this subsection shall be construed to require any creditor to be represented by an attorney at any meeting of creditors.

(d) Prior to the conclusion of the meeting of creditors or equity security holders, the trustee shall orally examine the debtor to ensure that the debtor in a case under chapter 7 of this title is aware of—

(1) the potential consequences of seeking a discharge in bankruptcy, including   the effects on credit history;

(2) the debtor's ability to file a petition under a different chapter of this title;

(3) the effect of receiving a discharge of debts under this title; and

(4) the effect of reaffirming a debt, including the debtor's knowledge of the provisions of section 524 (d) of this title.

(e) Notwithstanding subsections (a) and (b), the court, on the request of a party in interest and after notice and a hearing, for cause may order that the United States trustee not convene a meeting of creditors or equity security holders if the debtor has filed a plan as to which the debtor solicited acceptances prior to the commencement of the case.

§ 362 Automatic Stay.

(a) Except as provided in subsection (b) of this section, a petition filed under section 301, 302, or 303 of this title, or an application filed under section 5(a)(3) of the Securities Investor Protection Act of 1970, operates as a stay, applicable to all entities, of —

(1) the commencement or continuation, including the issuance or employment of process, of a judicial, administrative, or other action or proceeding against the debtor that was or could have been commenced before the commencement of the case under this title, or to recover a claim against the debtor that arose before the

commencement of the case under this title;

(2) the enforcement, against the debtor or against property of the estate, of a judgment obtained before the commencement of the case under this title;

(3) any act to obtain possession of property of the estate or of property from the estate or to exercise control over property of the estate;

(4) any act to create, perfect, or enforce any lien against property of the estate;

(5) any act to create, perfect, or enforce against property of the debtor any lien to the extent that such lien secures a claim that arose before the commencement of the case under this title;

(6) any act to collect, assess, or recover a claim against the debtor that arose before the commencement of the case under this title;

(7) the setoff of any debt owing to the debtor that arose before the commencement of the case under this title against any claim against the debtor; and

(8) the commencement or continuation of a proceeding before the United States Tax Court concerning a corporate debtor's tax liability for a taxable period the Bankruptcy Court may determine or concerning the tax liability of a debtor who is an individual for a taxable period ending before the date of the order for relief under this title.

    (b) The filing of a petition under section 301, 302, or 303 of this title, or of an application under section 5(a)(3) of the Securities Investor Protection Act of 1970, does not operate as a stay —

    (1) under subsection (a) of this section, of the commencement or continuation of a criminal action or proceeding against the debtor;

    (2) under subsection (a) —

        (A) of the commencement or continuation of a civil action or proceeding

            (i) for the establishment of paternity;

            (ii) for the establishment or modification of an order for domestic support obligations;

            (iii) concerning child custody or visitation;

            (iv) for the dissolution of a marriage, except to the extent that such proceeding seeks to determine the division of property that is property of the estate; or

            (v) regarding domestic violence;

        (B) of the collection of a domestic support obligation from property that is not property of the estate;

        (C) with respect to the withholding of income that is property of the estate or property of the debtor for payment of a domestic support obligation under a judicial or administrative order or a statute;

        (D) of the withholding, suspension, or restriction of a driver's license, a professional or occupational license, or a recreational license, under State law, as specified in section 466(a)(16) of the Social Security Act;

(E) of the reporting of overdue support owed by a parent to any consumer reporting agency as specified in section 466(a)(7) of the Social Security Act;

(F) of the interception of a tax refund, as specified in sections 464 and 466(a)(3) of the Social Security Act or under an analogous State law; or

(G) of the enforcement of a medical obligation, as specified under title IV of the Social Security Act;

(3) under subsection (a) of this section, of any act to perfect, or to maintain or continue the perfection of, an interest in property to the extent that the trustee's rights and powers are subject to such perfection under section 546(b) of this title or to the extent that such act is accomplished within the period provided under section 547(e)(2)(A) of this title;

(4) under paragraph (1), (2), (3), or (6) of subsection (a) of this section, of the commencement or continuation of an action or proceeding by a governmental unit or any organization exercising authority under the Convention on the Prohibition of the Development, Production, Stockpiling and Use of Chemical Weapons and on Their Destruction, opened for signature on January 13, 1993, to enforce such governmental unit's or organization's police and regulatory power, including the enforcement of a judgment other than a money judgment, obtained in an action or proceeding by the governmental unit to enforce such governmental unit's or organization's police or regulatory power;

(5) Repealed. Pub. L. 105-277, div. I, title VI, Sec. 603(1), Oct. 21, 1998, 112 Stat. 2681-886;

(6) under subsection (a) of this section, of the setoff by a commodity broker, forward contract merchant, stockbroker, financial institution, financial participant, or securities clearing agency of any mutual debt and claim under or in connection with commodity contracts, as defined in section 761 of this title, forward contracts, or securities contracts, as defined in section 741 of this title, that constitutes the setoff of a claim against the debtor for a margin payment, as defined in section 101, 741, or 761 of this title, or settlement payment, as defined in section 101 or 741 of this title, arising out of commodity contracts, forward contracts, or securities contracts against cash, securities, or other property held by, pledged to, under the control of, or due from such commodity broker, forward contract merchant, stockbroker, financial institution, financial participant, or securities clearing agency to margin, guarantee, secure, or settle commodity contracts, forward contracts, or securities contracts;

(7) under subsection (a) of this section, of the setoff by a repo participant or financial participant, of any mutual debt and claim under or in connection with repurchase agreements that constitutes the setoff of a claim against the debtor for a margin payment, as defined in section 741 or 761 of this title, or settlement payment, as defined in section 741 of this title, arising out of repurchase agreements against cash, securities, or other property held by, pledged to, under the control of, or due from such repo participant or financial participant to margin, guarantee, secure or settle repurchase agreements;

(8) under subsection (a) of this section, of the commencement of any action by the Secretary of Housing and Urban Development to foreclose a mortgage or deed of trust in any case in which the mortgage or deed of trust held by the Secretary is insured or was formerly insured under the National Housing Act and covers property, or combinations of property, consisting of five or more living units;

(9) under subsection (a), of —

    (A) an audit by a governmental unit to determine tax liability;

    (B) the issuance to the debtor by a governmental unit of a notice of tax deficiency;

    (C) a demand for tax returns; or

    (D) the making of an assessment for any tax and issuance of a notice and demand for payment of such an assessment (but any tax lien that would otherwise attach to property of the estate by reason of such an assessment shall not take effect unless such tax is a debt of the debtor that will not be discharged in the case and such property or its proceeds are transferred out of the estate to, or otherwise revested in, the debtor).

(10) under subsection (a) of this section, of any act by a lessor to the debtor under a lease of nonresidential real property that has terminated by the expiration of the stated term of the lease before the commencement of or during a case under this title to obtain possession of such property;

(11) under subsection (a) of this section, of the presentment of a negotiable instrument and the giving of notice of and protesting dishonor of such an instrument;

(12) under subsection (a) of this section, after the date which is 90 days after the filing of such petition, of the commencement or continuation, and conclusion to the entry of final judgment, of an action which involves a debtor subject to reorganization pursuant to chapter 11 of this title and which was brought by the Secretary of Transportation under section 31325 of title 46 (including distribution of any proceeds of sale) to foreclose a preferred ship or fleet mortgage, or a security interest in or relating to a vessel or vessel under construction, held by the Secretary of Transportation under section 207 or title XI of the Merchant Marine Act, 1936, or under applicable State law;

(13) under subsection (a) of this section, after the date which is 90 days after the filing of such petition, of the commencement or continuation, and conclusion to the entry of final judgment, of an action which involves a debtor subject to reorganization pursuant to chapter 11 of this title and which was brought by the Secretary of Commerce under section 31325 of title 46 (including distribution of any proceeds of sale) to foreclose a preferred ship or fleet mortgage in a vessel or a mortgage, deed of trust, or other security interest in a fishing facility held by the Secretary of Commerce under section 207 or title XI of the Merchant Marine Act, 1936;

(14) under subsection (a) of this section, of any action by an accrediting agency regarding the accreditation status of the debtor as an educational institution;

(15) under subsection (a) of this section, of any action by a State licensing body regarding the licensure of the debtor as an educational institution;

(16) under subsection (a) of this section, of any action by a guaranty agency, as defined in section 435(j) of the Higher Education Act of 1965 or the Secretary of Education regarding the eligibility of the debtor to participate in programs authorized under such Act;

(17) under subsection (a), of the setoff by a swap participant or financial participant of a mutual debt and claim under or in connection with one or more swap agreements that constitutes the setoff of a claim against the debtor for any payment or other transfer of property due from the debtor under or in connection with any swap agreement against any payment due to the debtor from the swap participant or financial participant under or in connection with any swap agreement or against cash, securities, or other property held by, pledged to, under the control of, or due from such swap participant or financial participant to margin, guarantee, secure, or settle any swap agreement;

(18) under subsection (a) of the creation or perfection of a statutory lien for an ad valorem property tax, or a special tax or special assessment on real property whether or not ad valorem, imposed by a governmental unit, if such tax or assessment comes due after the date of the filing of the petition;

(19) under subsection (a), of withholding of income from a debtor's wages and collection of amounts withheld, under the debtor's agreement authorizing that withholding and collection for the benefit of a pension, profit-sharing, stock bonus, or other plan established under section 401, 403, 408, 408A, 414, 457, or 501(c) of the Internal Revenue Code of 1986, that is sponsored by the employer of the debtor, or an affiliate, successor, or predecessor of such employer —

> **(A)** to the extent that the amounts withheld and collected are used solely for payments relating to a loan from a plan under section 408(b)(1) of the Employee Retirement Income Security Act of 1974 or is subject to section 72(p) of the Internal Revenue Code of 1986; or

(B) a loan from a thrift savings plan permitted under subchapter III of chapter 84 of title 5, that satisfies the requirements of section 8433(g) of such title; but nothing in this paragraph may be construed to provide that any loan made under a governmental plan under section 414(d), or a contract or account under section 403(b), of the Internal Revenue Code of 1986 constitutes a claim or a debt under this title;

(20) under subsection (a), of any act to enforce any lien against or security interest in real property following entry of the order under subsection (d)(4) as to such real property in any prior case under this title, for a period of 2 years after the date of the entry of such an order, except that the debtor, in a subsequent case under this title, may move for relief from such order based upon changed circumstances or for other good cause shown, after notice and a hearing;

(21) under subsection (a), of any act to enforce any lien against or security interest in real property —

(A) if the debtor is ineligible under section 109(g) to be a debtor in a case under this title; or

(B) if the case under this title was filed in violation of a Bankruptcy Court order in a prior case under this title prohibiting the debtor from being a debtor in another case under this title;

(22) subject to subsection (l), under subsection (a)(3), of the continuation of any eviction, unlawful detainer action, or similar proceeding by a lessor against a debtor involving residential property in which the debtor resides as a tenant under a lease or rental agreement and with respect to which the lessor has obtained before the date of the filing of the bankruptcy petition, a judgment for possession of such property against the debtor;

(23) subject to subsection (m), under subsection (a)(3), of an eviction action that seeks possession of the residential property in which the debtor resides as a tenant under a lease or rental agreement based on endangerment of such property or the illegal use of controlled substances on such property, but only if the lessor files with the court, and serves upon the debtor, a certification under penalty of perjury that such an eviction   action has been filed, or that the debtor, during the 30-day period preceding the date of the filing of the certification, has endangered property or illegally used or allowed to be used a controlled substance on the property;

(24) under subsection (a), of any transfer that is not avoidable under section 544 and that is not avoidable under section 549;

(25) under subsection (a), of —

(A) the commencement or continuation of an investigation or action by a securities self regulatory organization to enforce such organization's regulatory power;

(B) the enforcement of an order or decision, other than for monetary sanctions, obtained in an action by such securities self regulatory organization to enforce such organization's regulatory power; or

(C) any act taken by such securities self regulatory organization to delist, delete, or refuse to permit quotation of any stock that does not meet applicable regulatory requirements;

The provisions of paragraphs (12) and (13) of this subsection shall apply with respect to any such petition filed on or before December 31, 1989.

(26) under subsection (a), of the setoff under applicable nonbankruptcy law of an income tax refund, by a governmental unit, with respect to a taxable period that ended before the date of the order for relief against an income tax liability for a taxable period that also ended before the date of the order for relief, except that in any case in which the setoff of an income tax refund is not permitted under applicable nonbankruptcy law because of a pending action to determine the amount or legality of a tax liability, the governmental unit may hold the refund pending the resolution of the action, unless the court, on the motion of the trustee and after notice and a hearing, grants the taxing authority adequate protection (within the meaning of section 361) for the secured claim of such authority in the setoff under section 506(a);

(27) under subsection (a), of the setoff by a master netting agreement participant of a mutual debt and claim under or in connection with one or more master netting agreements or any contract or agreement subject to such agreements that constitutes the setoff of a claim against the debtor for any payment or other transfer of property due from the debtor under or in connection with such agreements or any contract or agreement subject to such agreements against any payment due to the debtor from such master netting agreement participant under or in connection with such agreements or any contract or agreement subject to such agreements or against cash, securities, or other property held by, pledged to, under the control of, or due from such master netting agreement participant to margin, guarantee, secure, or settle such agreements or any contract or agreement subject to such agreements, to the extent that such participant is eligible to exercise such offset rights under paragraph (6), (7), or (17) for each individual contract covered by the master netting agreement in issue; and

(28) under subsection (a), of the exclusion by the Secretary of Health and Human Services of the debtor from participation in the medicare program or any other Federal health care program (as defined in section 1128B(f) of the Social Security Act pursuant to title XI or XVIII of such Act).

(c) Except as provided in subsections (d), (e), (f), and (h) of this section

(1) the stay of an act against property of the estate under subsection (a) of this section continues until such property is no longer property of the estate;

(2) the stay of any other act under subsection (a) of this   section continues until the earliest of —

    (A) the time the case is closed;

    (B) the time the case is dismissed; or

    (C) if the case is a case under chapter 7 of this title concerning an individual or a case under chapter 9, 11, 12, or 13 of this title, the time a discharge is granted or denied;

(3) if a single or joint case is filed by or against debtor who is an individual in a case under chapter 7, 11, or 13, and if a single or joint case of the debtor was pending within the preceding 1-year period but was dismissed, other than a case refiled under a chapter other than chapter 7 after dismissal under section 707(b) —

    (A) the stay under subsection (a) with respect to any action taken with respect to a debt or property securing such debt or with respect to any lease shall terminate with respect to the debtor on the 30th day after the filing of the later case;

    (B) on the motion of a party in interest for continuation of the automatic stay and upon notice and a hearing, the court may extend the stay in particular cases as to any or all creditors (subject to such conditions or limitations as the court may then impose) after notice and a hearing completed before the expiration of the 30-day period only if the party in interest demonstrates that the filing of the later case is in good faith as to the creditors to be stayed; and

    (C) for purposes of subparagraph (B), a case is presumptively filed not in good faith (but such presumption may be rebutted by clear and convincing evidence to the contrary) —

        (i) as to all creditors, if —

        (I) more than 1 previous case under any of chapters 7, 11, and 13 in which the individual was a debtor was pending within the preceding 1-year period;

        (II) a previous case under any of chapters 7, 11, and 13 in which the individual was a debtor was dismissed within such 1-year period, after the debtor failed to —

            (aa) file or amend the petition or other documents as required by this title or the court without substantial excuse (but mere inadvertence or negligence shall not be a substantial excuse unless the dismissal was caused by the negligence of the debtor's attorney);

(bb) provide adequate protection as ordered by the court; or

(cc) perform the terms of a plan confirmed by the court; or

(III) there has not been a substantial change in the financial or personal affairs of the debtor since the dismissal of the next most previous case under chapter 7, 11, or 13 or any other reason to conclude that the later case will be concluded —

(aa) if a case under chapter 7, with a discharge; or

(bb) if a case under chapter 11 or 13, with a confirmed plan that will be fully performed; and

(ii) as to any creditor that commenced an action under

subsection (d) in a previous case in which the individual was a debtor if, as of the date of dismissal of such case, that action was still pending or had been resolved by terminating, conditioning, or limiting the stay as to actions of such creditor; and

(4)　　**(A)(i)** if a single or joint case is filed by or against a debtor who is an individual under this title, and if 2 or more single or joint cases of the debtor were pending within the previous year but were dismissed, other than a case refiled under section 707(b), the stay under subsection (a) shall not go into effect upon the filing of the later case; and

(ii) on request of a party in interest, the court shall promptly enter an order confirming that no stay is in effect;

(B) if, within 30 days after the filing of the later case, a party in interest requests the court may order the stay to take effect in the case as to any or all creditors (subject to such conditions or limitations as the court may impose), after notice and a hearing, only if the party in interest demonstrates that the filing of the later case is in good faith as to the creditors to be stayed;

(C) a stay imposed under subparagraph (B) shall be effective on the date of the entry of the order allowing the stay to go into effect; and

(D) for purposes of subparagraph (B), a case is presumptively filed not in good faith (but such presumption may be rebutted by clear and convincing evidence to the contrary) —

(i) as to all creditors if —

(I) 2 or more previous cases under this title in which the individual was a debtor were pending within the 1-year period;

(II) a previous case under this title in which the individual was a debtor was dismissed within the time period stated in this paragraph after the debtor failed to file or amend the petition or other documents as required by this title or the court without substantial excuse (but mere inadvertence or negligence shall not be substantial excuse unless the dismissal was caused by the negligence of the debtor's attorney), failed to provide adequate protection as ordered by the court, or failed to perform the terms of a plan confirmed by the court; or

(III) there has not been a substantial change in the financial or personal affairs of the debtor since the dismissal of the next most previous case under this title, or any other reason to conclude that the later case will not be concluded, if a case under chapter 7, with a discharge, and if a case under chapter 11 or 13, with a confirmed plan that will be fully performed; or

(ii) as to any creditor that commenced an action under subsection (d) in a previous case in which the individual was a debtor if, as of the date of dismissal of such case, such action was still pending or had been resolved by terminating, conditioning, or limiting the stay as to such action of such creditor.

(d) On request of a party in interest and after notice and a hearing, the court shall grant relief from the stay provided under subsection (a) of this section, such as by terminating, annulling, modifying, or conditioning such stay —

(1) for cause, including the lack of adequate protection of an interest in property of such party in interest;

(2) with respect to a stay of an act against property under subsection (a) of this section, if —

(A) the debtor does not have an equity in such property; and

(B) such property is not necessary to an effective reorganization;

(3) with respect to a stay of an act against single asset real estate under subsection (a), by a creditor whose claim is secured by an interest in such real estate, unless, not later than the date that is 90 days after the entry of the order for relief (or such later date as the court may determine for cause by order entered within that 90-day period) or 30 days after the court determines that the debtor is subject to this paragraph, whichever is later — (A) the debtor has filed a Plan of Reorganization that has a reasonable possibility of being confirmed within a reasonable time; or (B) the debtor has

commenced monthly payments that —

> **(i)** may, in the debtor's sole discretion, notwithstanding section 363(c)(2), be made from rents or other income generated before, on, or after the date of the commencement of the case by or from the property to each creditor whose claim is secured by such real estate (other than a claim secured by a judgment lien or by an unmatured statutory lien); and
>
> **(ii)** are in an amount equal to interest at the then applicable nondefault contract rate of interest on the value of the creditor's interest in the real estate; or

(4) with respect to a stay of an act against real property under subsection (a), by a creditor whose claim is secured by an interest in such real property, if the court finds that the filing of the petition was part of a scheme to delay, hinder, and defraud creditors that involved either —

> **(A)** transfer of all or part ownership of, or other interest in, such real property without the consent of the secured creditor or court approval; or
>
> **(B)** multiple bankruptcy filings affecting such real property.
>
> If recorded in compliance with applicable State laws governing notices of interests or liens in real property, an order entered under paragraph (4) shall be binding in any other case under this title purporting to affect such real property filed not later than 2 years after the date of the entry of such order by the court, except that a debtor in a subsequent case under this title may move for relief from such order based upon changed circumstances or for good cause shown, after notice and a hearing. Any Federal, State, or local governmental unit that accepts notices of interests or liens in real property shall accept any certified copy of an order described in this subsection for indexing and recording.

(e) **(1)** Thirty days after a request under subsection (d) of this section for relief from the stay of any act against property of the estate under subsection (a) of this section, such stay is terminated with respect to the party in interest making such request, unless the court, after notice and a hearing, orders such stay continued in effect pending the conclusion of, or as a result of, a final hearing and determination under subsection (d) of this section. A hearing under this subsection may be a preliminary hearing, or may be consolidated with the final hearing under subsection (d) of this section. The court shall order such stay continued in effect pending the conclusion of the final hearing under subsection (d) of this section if there is a reasonable likelihood that the party opposing relief from such stay will prevail at the conclusion of such final hearing. If the hearing under this subsection is a preliminary hearing, then such final hearing shall be concluded not later than thirty days after the conclusion of such preliminary hearing, unless the 30-day period is extended with the consent of the parties in interest or for a specific time which the court finds is required by compelling circumstances.

(2) Notwithstanding paragraph (1), in a case under chapter 7, 11, or 13 in which the debtor is an individual, the stay under subsection (a) shall terminate on the date that is 60 days after a request is made by a party in interest under subsection (d), unless —

(A) a final decision is rendered by the court during the 60-day period beginning on the date of the request; or

(B) such 60-day period is extended —

(i) by agreement of all parties in interest; or

(ii) by the court for such specific period of time as the court finds is required for good cause, as described in findings made by the court.

(f) Upon request of a party in interest, the court, with or without a hearing, shall grant such relief from the stay provided under subsection (a) of this section as is necessary to prevent irreparable damage to the interest of an entity in property, if such interest will suffer such damage before there is an opportunity for notice and a hearing under subsection (d) or (e) of this section.

(g) In any hearing under subsection (d) or (e) of this section concerning relief from the stay of any act under subsection (a) of this section —

(1) the party requesting such relief has the burden of proof on the issue of the debtor's equity in property; and

(2) the party opposing such relief has the burden of proof on all other issues.

(h)   **(1)** In a case in which the debtor is an individual, the stay provided by subsection (a) is terminated with respect to personal property of the estate or of the debtor securing in whole or in part a claim, or subject to an unexpired lease, and such personal property shall no longer be property of the estate if the debtor fails within the applicable time set by section 521(a)(2) —

(A) to file timely any statement of intention required under section 521(a)(2) with respect to such personal property or to indicate in such statement that the debtor will either surrender such personal property or retain it and, if retaining such personal property, either redeem such personal property pursuant to section 722, enter into an agreement of the kind specified in section 524c) applicable to the debt secured by such personal property, or assume such unexpired lease pursuant to section 365(p) if the trustee does not do so, as applicable; and

(B) to take timely the action specified in such statement, as it may be amended before expiration of the period for taking action, unless such statement specifies the debtor's intention to reaffirm such debt on the original contract terms and the creditor refuses to agree to the reaffirmation on such terms.

(2) Paragraph (1) does not apply if the court determines, on the motion of the trustee filed before the expiration of the applicable time set by section 521(a)(2), after notice and a hearing, that such personal property is of consequential value or benefit to the estate, and orders appropriate adequate protection of the creditor's interest, and orders the debtor to deliver any collateral in the debtor's possession to the trustee. If the court does not so determine, the stay provided by subsection (a) shall terminate upon the conclusion of the hearing on the motion.

(i) If a case commenced under chapter 7, 11, or 13 is dismissed due to the creation of a debt repayment plan, for purposes of subsection (c)(3), any subsequent case commenced by the debtor under any such chapter shall not be presumed to be filed not in good faith.

(j) On request of a party in interest, the court shall issue an order under subsection (c) confirming that the automatic stay has been terminated.

(k) **(1)** Except as provided in paragraph (2), an individual injured by any willful violation of a stay provided by this section shall recover actual damages, including costs and attorneys' fees, and, in appropriate circumstances, may recover punitive damages.

(2) If such violation is based on an action taken by an entity in the good faith belief that subsection (h) applies to the debtor, the recovery under paragraph (1) of this subsection against such entity shall be limited to actual damages.

(l) **(1)** Except as otherwise provided in this subsection, subsection (b)(22) shall apply on the date that is 30 days after the date on which the bankruptcy petition is filed, if the debtor files with the petition and serves upon the lessor a certification under penalty of perjury that —

(A) under nonbankruptcy law applicable in the jurisdiction, there are circumstances under which the debtor would be permitted to cure the entire monetary default that gave rise to the judgment for possession, after that judgment for possession was entered; and

(B) the debtor (or an adult dependent of the debtor) has deposited with the clerk of the court, any rent that would become due during the 30-day period after the filing of the bankruptcy petition.

(2) If, within the 30-day period after the filing of the bankruptcy petition, the debtor (or an adult dependent of the debtor) complies with paragraph (1) and files with the court and serves upon the lessor a further certification under penalty of perjury that the debtor (or an adult dependent of the debtor) has cured, under nonbankrupcty law applicable in the jurisdiction, the entire monetary default that gave rise to the judgment under which possession is sought by the lessor, subsection (b)(22) shall not apply, unless ordered to apply by the court under paragraph (3).

(3) **(A)** If the lessor files an objection to any certification filed by the debtor

under paragraph (1) or (2), and serves such objection upon the debtor, the court shall hold a hearing within 10 days after the filing and service of such objection to determine if the certification filed by the debtor under paragraph (1) or (2) is true.

(B) If the court upholds the objection of the lessor filed under subparagraph (A) —

(i) subsection (b)(22) shall apply immediately and relief from the stay provided under subsection (a)(3) shall not be required to enable the lessor to complete the process to recover full possession of the property; and

(ii) the clerk of the court shall immediately serve upon the lessor and the debtor a certified copy of the court's order upholding the lessor's objection.

(4) If a debtor, in accordance with paragraph (5), indicates on the petition that there was a judgment for possession of the residential rental property in which the debtor resides and does not file a certification under paragraph (1) or (2) —

(A) subsection (b)(22) shall apply immediately upon failure to file such certification, and relief from the stay provided under subsection (a)(3) shall not be required to enable the lessor to complete the process to recover full possession of the property; and

(B) the clerk of the court shall immediately serve upon the lessor and the debtor a certified copy of the docket indicating the absence of a filed certification and the applicability of the exception to the stay under subsection (b)(22).

(5) **(A)** Where a judgment for possession of residential property in which the debtor resides as a tenant under a lease or rental agreement has been obtained by the lessor, the debtor shall so indicate on the bankruptcy petition and shall provide the name and address of the lessor that obtained that pre-petition judgment on the petition and on any certification filed under this subsection.

(B) The form of certification filed with the petition, as specified in this subsection, shall provide for the debtor to certify, and the debtor shall certify —

(i) whether a judgment for possession of residential rental housing in which the debtor resides has been obtained against the debtor before the date of the filing of the petition; and

(ii) whether the debtor is claiming under paragraph

(1) that under nonbankruptcy law applicable in the jurisdiction, there are circumstances under which the debtor would be permitted to cure the entire monetary default that gave rise to the judgment for possession, after that judgment of possession was entered, and has made the appropriate deposit with the court.

(C) The standard forms (electronic and otherwise) used in a bankruptcy proceeding shall be amended to reflect the requirements of this subsection.

(D) The clerk of the court shall arrange for the prompt transmittal of the rent deposited in accordance with paragraph (1)(B) to the lessor.

(m)(1) Except as otherwise provided in this subsection, subsection (b)(23) shall apply on the date that is 15 days after the date on which the lessor files and serves a certification described in subsection (b)(23).

(2) **(A)** If the debtor files with the court an objection to the truth or legal sufficiency of the certification described in subsection (b)(23) and serves such objection upon the lessor, subsection (b)(23) shall not apply, unless ordered to apply by the court under this subsection.

(B) If the debtor files and serves the objection under subparagraph (A), the court shall hold a hearing within 10 days after the filing and service of such objection to determine if the situation giving rise to the lessor's certification under paragraph (1) existed or has been remedied.

(C) If the debtor can demonstrate to the satisfaction of the court that the situation giving rise to the lessor's certification under paragraph (1) did not exist or has been remedied, the stay provided under subsection (a)(3) shall remain in effect until the termination of the stay under this section.

(D) If the debtor cannot demonstrate to the satisfaction of the court that the situation giving rise to the lessor's certification under paragraph (1) did not exist or has been remedied —

(i) relief from the stay provided under subsection (a)(3) shall
not be required to enable the lessor to proceed with the eviction; and

(ii) the clerk of the court shall immediately serve upon the lessor and the debtor a certified copy of the court's order upholding the lessor's certification.

(3) If the debtor fails to file, within 15 days, an objection under paragraph (2)(A) —

(A) subsection (b)(23) shall apply immediately upon such failure and relief from the stay provided under subsection (a)(3) shall not be required to enable the lessor to complete the process to recover full possession of the property; and

(B) the clerk of the court shall immediately serve upon the lessor and the debtor a certified copy of the docket indicating such failure.

(n)(1) Except as provided in paragraph (2), subsection (a) does not apply in a case in which the debtor —

(A) is a debtor in a small business case pending at the time the petition is filed;

(B) was a debtor in a small business case that was dismissed for any reason by an order that became final in the 2-year period ending on the date of the order for relief entered with respect to the petition;

(C) was a debtor in a small business case in which a plan was confirmed in the 2-year period ending on the date of the order for relief entered with respect to the petition; or

(D) is an entity that has acquired substantially all of the assets or business of a small business debtor described in subparagraph (A), (B), or (C), unless such entity establishes by a preponderance of the evidence that such entity acquired substantially all of the assets or business of such small business debtor in good faith and not for the purpose of evading this paragraph.

(2) Paragraph (1) does not apply —

(A) to an involuntary case involving no collusion by the debtor with creditors; or

(B) to the filing of a petition if —

(i) the debtor proves by a preponderance of the evidence that the filing of the petition resulted from circumstances beyond the control of the debtor not foreseeable at the time the case then pending was filed; and

(ii) it is more likely than not that the court will confirm a feasible plan, but not a liquidating plan, within a reasonable period of time.

(o) The exercise of rights not subject to the stay arising under subsection (a) pursuant to paragraph (6), (7), (17), or (27) of subsection (b) shall not be stayed by any order of a court or administrative agency in any proceeding under this title.

§ 363 Use, Sale, or Lease of Property.

(a) In this section, "cash collateral" means cash, negotiable instruments, documents of title, securities, deposit accounts, or other cash equivalents whenever acquired in which the estate and an entity other than the estate have an interest and includes the proceeds, products, offspring, rents, or profits of property and the fees, charges, accounts or other payments for the use or occupancy of rooms and other public facilities in hotels, motels, or other lodging properties subject to a security interest as provided in section 552(b) of this title, whether existing before or after the commencement of a case under this title.

(b)(1) The trustee, after notice and a hearing, may use, sell, or lease, other than in the ordinary course of business, property of the estate, except that if the debtor in connection with offering a product or a service discloses to an individual a policy prohibiting the transfer of personally identifiable information about individuals to persons that are not affiliated with the debtor and if such policy is in effect on the date of the commencement of the case, then the trustee may not sell or lease personally identifiable information to any person unless —

(A) such sale or such lease is consistent with such policy; or

(B) after appointment of a consumer privacy ombudsman in accordance with section 332, and after notice and a hearing, the court approves such sale or such lease —

(i) giving due consideration to the facts, circumstances, and conditions of such sale or such lease; and

(ii) finding that no showing was made that such sale or such lease would violate applicable nonbankruptcy law.

(2) If notification is required under subsection (a) of section 7A of the Clayton Act in the case of a transaction under this subsection, then —

(A) notwithstanding subsection (a) of such section, the notification required by such subsection to be given by the debtor shall be given by the trustee; and

(B) notwithstanding subsection (b) of such section, the required waiting period shall end on the 15th day after the date of the receipt, by the Federal Trade Commission and the Assistant Attorney General in charge of the Antitrust Division of the Department of Justice, of the notification required under such subsection (a), unless such waiting period is extended —

(i) pursuant to subsection (e)(2) of such section, in the same manner as such subsection (e)(2) applies to a cash tender offer;

(ii) pursuant to subsection (g)(2) of such section; or

(iii) by the court after notice and a hearing.

(c) (1) If the business of the debtor is authorized to be operated under section 721, 1108, 1203, 1204, or 1304 of this title and unless the court orders otherwise, the trustee may enter into transactions, including the sale or lease of property of the estate, in the ordinary course of business, without notice or a hearing, and may use property of the estate in the ordinary course of business without notice or a hearing.

(2) The trustee may not use, sell, or lease cash collateral under paragraph (1) of this subsection unless —

> **(A)** each entity that has an interest in such cash collateral consents; or
>
> **(B)** the court, after notice and a hearing, authorizes such use, sale, or lease in accordance with the provisions of this section.

(3) Any hearing under paragraph (2)(B) of this subsection may be a preliminary hearing or may be consolidated with a hearing under subsection (e) of this section, but shall be scheduled in accordance with the needs of the debtor. If the hearing under paragraph (2)(B) of this subsection is a preliminary hearing, the court may authorize such use, sale, or lease only if there is a reasonable likelihood that the trustee will prevail at the final hearing under subsection (e) of this section. The court shall act promptly on any request for authorization under paragraph (2)(B) of this subsection.

(4) Except as provided in paragraph (2) of this subsection, the trustee shall segregate and account for any cash collateral in the trustee's possession, custody, or control.

(d) The trustee may use, sell, or lease property under subsection (b) or (c) of this section only —

> **(1)** in accordance with applicable nonbankruptcy law that governs the transfer of property by a corporation or trust that is not a moneyed, business, or commercial corporation or trust; and
>
> **(2)** to the extent not inconsistent with any relief granted under subsection (c), (d), (e), or (f) of section 362.

(e) Notwithstanding any other provision of this section, at any time, on request of an entity that has an interest in property used, sold, or leased, or proposed to be used, sold, or leased, by the trustee, the court, with or without a hearing, shall prohibit or condition such use, sale, or lease as is necessary to provide adequate protection of such interest. This subsection also applies to property that is subject to any unexpired lease of personal property (to the exclusion of such property being subject to an order to grant relief from the stay under section 362).

(f) The trustee may sell property under subsection (b) or (c) of this section free and clear of any interest in such property of an entity other than the estate, only if —

> **(1)** applicable nonbankruptcy law permits sale of such property free and clear of such interest;
>
> **(2)** such entity consents;
>
> **(3)** such interest is a lien and the price at which such property is to be sold is greater than the aggregate value of all liens on such property;
>
> **(4)** such interest is in bona fide dispute; or
>
> **(5)** such entity could be compelled, in a legal or equitable proceeding, to accept a money satisfaction of such interest.

(g) Notwithstanding subsection (f) of this section, the trustee may sell property under subsection (b) or (c) of this section free and clear of any vested or contingent right in the nature of dower or courtesy.

(h) Notwithstanding subsection (f) of this section, the trustee may sell both the estate's interest, under subsection (b) or (c) of this section, and the interest of any co-owner in property in which the debtor had, at the time of the commencement of the case, an undivided interest as a tenant in common, joint tenant, or tenant by the entirety, only if —

> **(1)** partition in kind of such property among the estate and such co-owners is impracticable;
>
> **(2)** sale of the estate's undivided interest in such property would realize significantly less for the estate than sale of such property free of the interests of such co-owners;
>
> **(3)** the benefit to the estate of a sale of such property free of the interests of co-owners outweighs the detriment, if any, to such co-owners; and
>
> **(4)** such property is not used in the production, transmission, or distribution, for sale, of electric energy or of natural or synthetic gas for heat, light, or power.

(i) Before the consummation of a sale of property to which subsection (g) or (h) of this section applies, or of property of the estate that was community property of the debtor and the debtor's spouse immediately before the commencement of the case, the debtor's spouse, or a co-owner of such property, as the case may be, may purchase such property at the price at which such sale is to be consummated.

(j) After a sale of property to which subsection (g) or (h) of this section applies, the trustee shall distribute to the debtor's spouse or the co-owners of such property, as the case may be, and to the estate, the proceeds of such sale, less the costs and expenses, not including any compensation of the trustee, of such sale, according to the interests of such spouse or co-owners, and of the estate.

(k) At a sale under subsection (b) of this section of property that is subject to a lien that secures an allowed claim, unless the court for cause orders otherwise the holder of such claim may bid at such sale, and, if the holder of such claim purchases such property, such holder may offset such claim against the purchase price of such property.

(l) Subject to the provisions of section 365, trustee may use, sell, or lease property under subsection (b) or (c) of this section, or a plan under chapter 11, 12, or 13 of this title may provide for the use, sale, or lease of property, notwithstanding any provision in a contract, a lease, or applicable law that is conditioned on the insolvency or financial condition of the debtor, on the commencement of a case under this title concerning the debtor, or on the appointment of or the taking possession by a trustee in a case under this title or a custodian, and that effects, or gives an option to effect, a forfeiture, modification, or termination of the debtor's interest in such property.

(m) The reversal or modification on appeal of an authorization under subsection (b) or (c) of this section of a sale or lease of property does not affect the validity of a sale or lease under such authorization to an entity that purchased or leased such property in good faith, whether or not such entity knew of the pendency of the appeal, unless such authorization and such sale or lease were   stayed pending appeal.

(n) The trustee may avoid a sale under this section if the sale price was controlled by an agreement among potential bidders at such sale, or may recover from a party to such agreement any amount by which the value of the property sold exceeds the price at which such sale was consummated, and may recover any costs, attorneys' fees, or expenses incurred in avoiding such sale or recovering such amount. In addition to any recovery under the preceding sentence, the court may grant judgment for punitive damages in favor of the estate and against any such party that entered into such an agreement in willful disregard of this subsection.

(o) Notwithstanding subsection (f), if a person purchases any interest in a consumer credit transaction that is subject to the Truth in Lending Act or any interest in a consumer credit contract (as defined in section 433.1 of title 16 of the Code of Federal Regulations (January 1, 2004), as amended from time to time), and if such interest is purchased through a sale under this section, then such person shall remain subject to all claims and defenses that are related to such consumer credit transaction or such consumer credit contract, to the same extent as such person would be subject to such claims and defenses of the consumer had such interest been purchased at a sale not under this section.

(p) In any hearing under this section

(1) the trustee has the burden of proof on the issue of adequate protection; and

(2) the entity asserting an interest in property has the burden of proof on the issue of the validity, priority, or extent of such interest.

§ 364 Obtaining Credit.

(a) If the trustee is authorized to operate the business of the debtor court orders otherwise, the trustee may obtain unsecured credit and incur unsecured debt in the ordinary course of business allowable under section 503(b)(1) of this title as an administrative expense.

(b) The court, after notice and a hearing, may authorize the trustee to obtain unsecured credit or to incur unsecured debt other than under subsection (a) of this section, allowable under section 503(b)(1) of this title as an administrative expense.

(c) If the trustee is unable to obtain unsecured credit allowable under section 503(b)(1) of this title as an administrative expense, the court, after notice and a hearing, may authorize the obtaining of credit or the incurring of debt —

(1) with priority over any or all administrative expenses of the kind specified in section 503(b) or 507(b) of this title;

(2) secured by a lien on property of the estate that is not otherwise subject to a lien; or

(3) secured by a junior lien on property of the estate that is subject to a lien.

(d)   (1) The court, after notice and a hearing, may authorize the obtaining of credit or the incurring of debt secured by a senior or equal lien on property of the estate that is subject to a lien only if —

> **(A)** the trustee is unable to obtain such credit otherwise; and
>
> **(B)** there is adequate protection of the interest of the holder of the lien on the property of the estate on which such senior or equal lien is proposed to be granted.

(2) In any hearing under this subsection, the trustee has the burden of proof on the issue of adequate protection.

(e) The reversal or modification on appeal of an authorization under this section to obtain credit or incur debt, or of a grant under this section of a priority or a lien, does not affect the validity of any debt so incurred, or any priority or lien so granted, to an entity that extended such credit in good faith, whether or not such entity knew of the pendency of the appeal, unless such authorization and the incurring of such debt, or the granting of such priority or lien, were stayed pending appeal.

(f) Except with respect to an entity that is an underwriter as defined in section 1145(b) of this title, section 5 of the Securities Act of 1933, the Trust Indenture Act of 1939, and any State or local law requiring registration for offer or sale of a security or registration or licensing of an issuer of, underwriter of, or broker or dealer in, a security does not an equity security.

§ 365 Executory Contracts and Unexpired Leases.

(a) Except as provided in sections 765 and 766 of this title and in subsections (b), (c), and (d) of this section, the trustee, subject to the court's approval, may assume or reject any executory contract or unexpired lease of the debtor.

(b)   (1) If there has been a default in an executory contract or unexpired lease of the debtor, the trustee may not assume such contract or lease unless, at the time of assumption of such contract or lease, the trustee —

> **(A)** cures, or provides adequate assurance that the trustee will promptly cure, such default other than a default that is a breach of a provision relating to the satisfaction of any provision (other than a penalty rate or penalty provision) relating to a default arising from any failure to perform nonmonetary obligations under an unexpired lease of real property,
>
> if it is impossible for the trustee to cure such default by performing nonmonetary acts at and after the time of assumption, except that if such default arises from a failure to operate in accordance with a nonresidential real property lease, then such default shall be cured by performance at and after the time of assumption in accordance with such lease, and pecuniary losses resulting from such default shall be compensated in accordance with the provisions of this paragraph;
>
> **(B)** compensates, or provides adequate assurance that

the trustee will promptly compensate, a party other than the debtor to such contract or lease, for any actual pecuniary loss to such party resulting from such default; and

(C) provides adequate assurance of future performance under such contract or lease.

(2) Paragraph (1) of this subsection does not apply to a default that is a breach of a provision relating to —

(A) the insolvency or financial condition of the debtor at any time before the closing of the case;

(B) the commencement of a case under this title;

(C) the appointment of or taking possession by a trustee in a case under this title or a custodian before such commencement; or

(D) the satisfaction of any penalty rate or penalty provision relating to a default arising from any failure by the debtor to perform nonmonetary obligations under the executory contract or unexpired lease.

(3) For the purposes of paragraph (1) of this subsection and paragraph (2)(B) of subsection (f), adequate assurance of future performance of a lease of real property in a shopping center includes adequate assurance —

(A) of the source of rent and other consideration due under such lease, and in the case of an assignment, that the financial condition and operating performance of the proposed assignee and its guarantors, if any, shall be similar to the financial condition and operating performance of the debtor and its guarantors, if any, as of the time the debtor became the lessee under the lease;

(B) that any percentage rent due under such lease will not decline substantially;

(C) that assumption or assignment of such lease is subject to all the provisions thereof, including (but not limited to) provisions such as a radius, location, use, or exclusivity provision, and will not breach any such provision contained in any other lease, financing agreement, or master agreement relating to such shopping center; and

(D) that assumption or assignment of such lease will not disrupt any tenant mix or balance in such shopping center.

(4) Notwithstanding any other provision of this section, if there has been a default in an unexpired lease of the debtor, other than a default of a kind specified in paragraph (2) of this subsection, the trustee may not require a lessor to provide services or supplies incidental to such lease before assumption of such lease unless the lessor is compensated under the terms of such lease for any services and supplies provided under such lease before assumption of such lease.

(c) The trustee may not assume or assign any executory contract or unexpired lease of the debtor, whether or not such contract or lease prohibits or restricts assignment of rights or delegation of duties, if —

    (1)   **(A)** applicable law excuses a party, other than the debtor, to such contract or lease from accepting performance from or rendering performance to an entity other than the debtor or the debtor in possession, whether or not such contract or lease prohibits or restricts assignment of rights or delegation of duties; and

    (B) such party does not consent to such assumption or assignment; or

    (2) such contract is a contract to make a loan, or extend other debt financing or financial accommodations, to or for the benefit of the debtor, or to issue a security of the debtor; or

    (3) such lease is of nonresidential real property and has been terminated under applicable nonbankruptcy law prior to the order for relief.

(d)   **(1)** In a case under chapter 7 of this title, if the trustee does not assume or reject an executory contract or unexpired lease of residential real property or of personal property of the debtor within 60 days after the order for relief, or within such additional time as the court, for cause, within such 60-day period, fixes, then such contract or lease is deemed rejected.

(2) In a case under chapter 9, 11, 12, or 13 of this title, the trustee may assume or reject an executory contract or unexpired lease of residential real property or of personal property of the debtor at any time before the confirmation of a plan but the court, on the request of any party to such contract or lease, may order the trustee to determine within a specified period of time whether to assume or reject such contract or lease.

(3) The trustee shall timely perform all the obligations of the debtor, except those specified in section 365(b)(2), arising from and after the order for relief under any unexpired lease of nonresidential real property, until such lease is assumed or rejected, notwithstanding section 503(b)(1) of this title. The court may extend, for cause, the time for performance of any such obligation that arises within 60 days after the date of the order for relief, but the time for performance shall not be extended beyond such 60-day period. This subsection shall not be deemed to affect the trustee's obligations under the provisions of subsection (b) or (f) of this section. Acceptance of any such performance does not constitute waiver or relinquishment of the lessor's rights under such lease or under this title.

    (4)   **(A)** Subject to subparagraph (B), an unexpired lease of nonresidential real property under which the debtor is the lessee shall be deemed rejected, and the trustee shall immediately surrender that nonresidential real property to the lessor, if the trustee does not assume or reject the unexpired lease by the earlier of —

(i) the date that is 120 days after the date of the order for relief; or

(ii) the date of the entry of an order confirming a plan.

(B)(i) The court may extend the period determined under subparagraph (A), prior to the expiration of the 120-day period, for 90 days on the motion of the trustee or lessor for cause.   (ii) If the court grants an extension under clause (i), the court may grant a subsequent extension only upon prior written consent of the lessor in each instance.

(5) The trustee shall timely perform all of the obligations of the debtor, except those specified in section 365(b)(2), first arising from or after 60 days after the order for relief in a case under chapter 11 of this title under an unexpired lease of personal property (other than personal property leased to an individual primarily for personal, family, or household purposes), until such lease is assumed or rejected notwithstanding section 503(b)(1) of this title, unless the court, after notice and a hearing and based on the equities of the case, orders otherwise with respect to the obligations or timely performance thereof. This subsection shall not be deemed to affect the trustee's obligations under the provisions of subsection (b) or (f). Acceptance of any such performance does not constitute waiver or relinquishment of the lessor's rights under such lease or under this title.

(e)(1) Notwithstanding a provision in an executory contract or unexpired lease, or in applicable law, an executory contract or unexpired lease of the debtor may not be terminated or modified, and any right or obligation under such contract or lease may not be terminated or modified, at any time after the commencement of the case solely because of a provision in such contract or lease that is conditioned on —

(A) the insolvency or financial condition of the debtor at any time before the closing of the case;

(B) the commencement of a case under this title; or

(C) the appointment of or taking possession by a trustee in a case under this title or a custodian before such commencement.

(2) Paragraph (1) of this subsection does not apply to an executory contract or unexpired lease of the debtor, whether or not such contract or lease prohibits or restricts assignment of rights or delegation of duties, if —

(A)(i) applicable law excuses a party, other than the debtor, to such contract or lease from accepting performance from or rendering performance to the trustee or to an assignee of such contract or lease, whether or not such contract or lease prohibits or restricts assignment of rights or delegation of duties; and

(ii) such party does not consent to such assumption or

assignment; or

(B) such contract is a contract to make a loan, or extend other debt financing or financial accommodations, to or for the benefit of the debtor, or to issue a security of the debtor.

(f) **(1)** Except as provided in subsections (b) and (c) of this section, notwithstanding a provision in an executory contract or unexpired lease of the debtor, or in applicable law, that prohibits, restricts, or conditions the assignment of such contract or lease, the trustee may assign such contract or lease under paragraph **(2)** of (2) The trustee may assign an

executory contract or unexpired lease of the debtor only if —

(A) the trustee assumes such contract or lease in accordance with the provisions of this section; and

(B) adequate assurance of future performance by the assignee of such contract or lease is provided, whether or not there has been a default in such contract or lease.

(3) Notwithstanding a provision in an executory contract or unexpired lease of the debtor, or in applicable law that terminates or modifies, or permits a party other than the debtor to terminate or modify, such contract or lease or a right or obligation under such contract or lease on account of an assignment of such contract or lease, such contract, lease, right, or obligation may not be terminated or modified under such provision because of the assumption or assignment of such contract or lease by the trustee.

(g) Except as provided in subsections (h)(2) and (i)(2) of this section, the rejection of an executory contract or unexpired lease of the debtor constitutes a breach of such contract or lease —

(1) if such contract or lease has not been assumed under this section or under a plan confirmed under chapter 9, 11, 12, or 13 of this title, immediately before the date of the filing of the petition; or

(2) if such contract or lease has been assumed under this section or under a plan confirmed under chapter 9, 11, 12, or 13 of this title —

(A) if before such rejection the case has not been converted under section 1112, 1208, or 1307 of this title, at the time of such rejection; or

(B) if before such rejection the case has been converted under section 1112, 1208, or 1307 of this title —

(i) immediately before the date of such conversion, if such contract or lease was assumed before such conversion; or

(ii) at the time of such rejection, if such contract or lease was assumed after such conversion.

(h) **(1)(A)** If the trustee rejects an unexpired lease of real property under which the debtor is the lessor and —

(i) if the rejection by the trustee amounts to such a breach as would entitle the lessee to treat such lease as terminated by virtue of its terms, applicable nonbankruptcy law, or any agreement made by the lessee, then the lessee under such lease may treat such lease as terminated by the rejection; or

(ii) if the term of such lease has commenced, the lessee may retain its rights under such lease (including rights such as those relating to the amount and timing of payment of rent and other amounts payable by the lessee and any right of use, possession, quiet enjoyment, subletting, assignment, or hypothecation) that are in or appurtenant to the real property for the balance of the term of such lease and for any renewal or extension of such rights to the extent that such rights are enforceable under applicable nonbankruptcy law.

(B) If the lessee retains its rights under subparagraph (A)(ii),the lessee may offset against the rent reserved under such lease for the balance of the term after the date of the rejection of such lease and for the term of any renewal or extension of such lease, the value of any damage caused by the nonperformance after the date of such rejection, of any obligation of the debtor under such lease, but the lessee shall not have any other right against the estate or the debtor on account of any damage occurring after such date caused by such nonperformance.

(C) The rejection of a lease of real property in a shopping center with respect to which the lessee elects to retain its rights under subparagraph (A)(ii) does not affect the enforceability under applicable nonbankruptcy law of any provision in the lease pertaining to radius, location, use, exclusivity, or tenant mix or balance.

(D) In this paragraph, "lessee" includes any successor, assign, or mortgagee permitted under the terms of such lease.

(2)   (A) If the trustee rejects a timeshare interest under a timeshare plan under which the debtor is the timeshare interest seller and —

(i) if the rejection amounts to such a breach as would entitle the timeshare interest purchaser to treat the timeshare plan as terminated under its terms, applicable nonbankruptcy law, or any agreement made by timeshare interest purchaser, the timeshare interest purchaser under the timeshare plan may treat the timeshare plan as terminated by such rejection; or

(ii) if the term of such timeshare interest has commenced, then the timeshare interest purchaser may retain its rights in such timeshare interest for the balance of such term and for any term of renewal or extension of such timeshare interest to the extent that such rights are enforceable under applicable nonbankruptcy law.

(B) If the timeshare interest purchaser retains its rights under subparagraph (A), such timeshare interest purchaser may offset against the moneys due for such timeshare interest for the balance of the term after the date of the rejection of such timeshare interest, and the term of any renewal or extension of such timeshare interest, the value of any damage caused by the nonperformance after the date of such rejection, of any obligation of the debtor under such timeshare plan, but the timeshare interest purchaser shall not have any right against the estate or the debtor on account of any damage occurring after such date caused by such nonperformance.

(i) (1) If the trustee rejects an executory contract of the debtor for the sale of real property or for the sale of a timeshare interest under a timeshare plan, under which the purchaser is in possession, such purchaser may treat such contract as terminated, or, in the alternative, may remain in possession of such real property or timeshare interest.

(2) If such purchaser remains in possession —

(A) such purchaser shall continue to make all payments due under such contract, but may, offset against such payments any damages occurring after the date of the rejection of such contract caused by the nonperformance of any obligation of the debtor after such date, but such purchaser does not have any rights against the estate on account of any damages arising after such date from such rejection, other than such offset; and

(B) the trustee shall deliver title to such purchaser in accordance with the provisions of such contract, but is relieved of all other obligations to perform under such contract.

(j) A purchaser that treats an executory contract as terminated under subsection (i) of this section, or a party whose executory contract to purchase real property from the debtor is rejected and under which such party is not in possession, has a lien on the interest of the debtor in such property for the recovery of any portion of the purchase price that such purchaser or party has paid.

(k) Assignment by the trustee to an entity of a contract or lease assumed under this section relieves the trustee and the estate from any liability for any breach of such contract or lease occurring after such assignment.

(l) If an unexpired lease under which the debtor is the lessee is assigned pursuant to this section, the lessor of the property may require a deposit or other security for the performance of the debtor's obligations under the lease substantially the same as would have been required by the landlord upon the initial leasing to a similar tenant.

(m) For purposes of this section 365 and sections 541(b)(2) and 362(b)(10), leases of real property shall include any rental agreement to use real property.

(n)(1) If the trustee rejects an executory contract under which the debtor is a licensor of a right to intellectual property, the licensee under such contract may elect —

(A) to treat such contract as terminated by such rejection if such rejection by the trustee amounts to such a breach as would entitle the licensee to treat such contract as terminated by virtue of its own terms, applicable nonbankruptcy law, or an agreement made by the licensee with another entity; or

(B) to retain its rights (including a right to enforce any exclusivity provision of such contract, but excluding any other right under applicable nonbankruptcy law to specific performance of such contract) under such contract and under any agreement supplementary to such contract, to such intellectual property (including any embodiment of such intellectual property to the extent protected by applicable nonbankruptcy law), as such rights existed immediately before the case commenced, for —

(i) the duration of such contract; and

(ii) any period for which such contract may be extended by the licensee as of right under applicable nonbankruptcy law.

(2) If the licensee elects to retain its rights, as described in paragraph (1)(B) of this subsection, under such contract —

(A) the trustee shall allow the licensee to exercise such rights;

(B) the licensee shall make all royalty payments due under such contract for the duration of such contract and for any period described in paragraph (1)(B) of this subsection for which the licensee extends such contract; and

(C) the licensee shall be deemed to waive —

(i) any right of setoff it may have with respect to such contract under this title or applicable nonbankruptcy law; and

(ii) any claim allowable under section 503(b) of this title arising from the performance of such contract.

(3) If the licensee elects to retain its rights, as described in paragraph (1)(B) of this subsection, then on the written request of the licensee the trustee shall —

    (A) to the extent provided in such contract, or any agreement supplementary to such contract, provide to the licensee any intellectual property (including such embodiment) held by the trustee; and

    (B) not interfere with the rights of the licensee as provided in such contract, or any agreement supplementary to such contract, to such intellectual property (including such embodiment) including any right to obtain such intellectual property (or such embodiment) from another entity.

(4) Unless and until the trustee rejects such contract, on the written request of the licensee the trustee shall —

    (A) to the extent provided in such contract or any agreement supplementary to such contract —

        (i) perform such contract; or

        (ii) provide to the licensee such intellectual property (including any embodiment of such intellectual property to the extent protected by applicable nonbankruptcy law) held by the trustee; and

    (B) not interfere with the rights of the licensee as provided in such contract, or any agreement supplementary to such contract, to such intellectual property (including such embodiment), including any right to obtain such intellectual property (or such embodiment) from another entity.

(o) In a case under chapter 11 of this title, the trustee shall be deemed to have assumed (consistent with the debtor's other obligations under section 507), and shall immediately cure any deficit under, any commitment by the debtor to a Federal depository institutions regulatory agency (or predecessor to such agency) to maintain the capital of an insured depository institution, and any claim for a subsequent breach of the obligations thereunder shall be entitled to priority under section 507. This subsection shall not extend any commitment that would otherwise be terminated by any act of such an agency.

(p) **(1)** If a lease of personal property is rejected or not timely assumed by the trustee under subsection (d), the leased property is no longer property of the estate and the stay under section 362(a) is automatically terminated.

    (2)   **(A)** If the debtor in a case under chapter 7 is an individual, the debtor may notify the creditor in writing that the debtor desires to assume the lease. Upon being so notified, the creditor may, at its option, notify the debtor that it is willing to have the lease assumed by the debtor and may condition such assumption on cure of any outstanding default on terms set by the contract.

        (B) If, not later than 30 days after notice is provided under subparagraph (A), the debtor notifies the lessor in writing that the lease is assumed, the liability under the lease will be assumed by the debtor and not by the estate.

(C) The stay under section 362 and the injunction under section 524(a)(2) shall not be violated by notification of the debtor and negotiation of cure under this subsection.

(3) In a case under chapter 11 in which the debtor is an individual and in a case under chapter 13, if the debtor is the lessee with respect to personal property and the lease is not assumed in the plan confirmed by the court, the lease is deemed rejected as of the conclusion of the hearing on confirmation. If the lease is rejected, the stay under section 362 and any stay under section 1301 is automatically terminated with respect to the property subject to the lease.

§ 501 Filing proofs of claims or interests

(a) A creditor or an indenture trustee may file a proof of claim. An equity security holder may file a proof of interest.

(b) If a creditor does not timely file a proof of such creditor's claim, an entity that is liable to such creditor with the debtor, or that has secured such creditor, may file a proof of such claim.

(c) If a creditor does not timely file a proof of such creditor's claim, the debtor or the trustee may file a proof of such claim.

(d) A claim of a kind specified in section 502 (e)(2), 502 (f), 502 (g), 502 (h) or 502 (i) of this title may be filed under subsection (a), (b), or (c) of this section the same as if such claim were a claim against the debtor and had arisen before the date of the filing of the petition.

(e) A claim arising from the liability of the debtor for fuel use tax assessed consistent with the requirements of section 31705 of title 49 may be filed by the base jurisdiction designated pursuant to the International Fuel Tax Agreement (as defined in section 31701 of title 49) and, if so filed, shall be allowed as a single claim.

§ 502 Allowance of claims or interests

(a) A claim or interest, proof of which is filed under section 501 of this title, is deemed allowed, unless a party in interest, including a creditor of a general partner in a partnership that is a debtor in a case under chapter 7 of this title, objects.

(b) Except as provided in subsections (e)(2), (f), (g), (h) and (i) of this section, if such objection to a claim is made, the court, after notice and a hearing, shall determine the amount of such claim in lawful currency of the United States as of the date of the filing of the petition, and shall allow such claim in such amount, except to the extent that—

> **(1)** such claim is unenforceable against the debtor and property of the debtor, under any agreement or applicable law for a reason other than because such claim is contingent or unmatured;
>
> **(2)** such claim is for unmatured interest;
>
> **(3)** if such claim is for a tax assessed against property of the estate, such claim exceeds the value of the interest of the estate in such property;

(4) if such claim is for services of an insider or attorney of the debtor, such claim exceeds the reasonable value of such services;

(5) such claim is for a debt that is unmatured on the date of the filing of the petition and that is excepted from discharge under section 523 (a)(5) of this title;

(6) if such claim is the claim of a lessor for damages resulting from the termination of a lease of real property, such claim exceeds—

> **(A)** the rent reserved by such lease, without acceleration, for the greater of one year, or 15 percent, not to exceed three years, of the remaining term of such lease, following the earlier of—
>
>> **(i)** the date of the filing of the petition; and
>> **(ii)** the date on which such lessor repossessed, or the lessee surrendered, the leased property; plus
>
> **(B)** any unpaid rent due under such lease, without acceleration, on the earlier of such dates;

(7) if such claim is the claim of an employee for damages resulting from the termination of an employment contract, such claim exceeds—

> **(A)** the compensation provided by such contract, without acceleration, for one year following the earlier of—
>
>> **(i)** the date of the filing of the petition; or
>> **(ii)** the date on which the employer directed the employee to terminate, or such employee terminated, performance under such contract; plus
>
> **(B)** any unpaid compensation due under such contract, without acceleration, on the earlier of such dates;

(8) such claim results from a reduction, due to late payment, in the amount of an otherwise applicable credit available to the debtor in connection with an employment tax on wages, salaries, or commissions earned from the debtor; or

(9) proof of such claim is not timely filed, except to the extent tardily filed as permitted under paragraph (1), (2), or (3) of section 726 (a) of this title or under the Federal Rules of Bankruptcy Procedure, except that a claim of a governmental unit shall be timely filed if it is filed before 180 days after the date of the order for relief or such later time as the Federal Rules of Bankruptcy Procedure may provide and except that in a case under Chapter 13 , a claim of a governmental unit for a tax with respect to a return filed under Section 1308 shall be timely if the claim is filed on or before the date that is 60 days after the date on which such return was filed as required.

(c) There shall be estimated for purpose of allowance under this section—

> **(1)** any contingent or unliquidated claim, the fixing or liquidation of which, as the case may be, would unduly delay the administration of the case; or

(2) any right to payment arising from a right to an equitable remedy for breach of performance.

(d) Notwithstanding subsections (a) and (b) of this section, the court shall disallow any claim of any entity from which property is recoverable under section 542, 543, 550, or 553 of this title or that is a transferee of a transfer avoidable under section 522 (f), 522 (h), 544, 545, 547, 548, 549, or 724 (a) of this title, unless such entity or transferee has paid the amount, or turned over any such property, for which such entity or transferee is liable under section 522 (i), 542, 543, 550, or 553 of this title.

> **(e)** **(1)** Notwithstanding subsections (a), (b), and (c) of this section and paragraph (2) of this subsection, the court shall disallow any claim for reimbursement or contribution of an entity that is liable with the debtor on or has secured the claim of a creditor, to the extent that—
>
>> **(A)** such creditor's claim against the estate is disallowed;
>> **(B)** such claim for reimbursement or contribution is contingent as of the time of allowance or disallowance of such claim for reimbursement or contribution; or
>> **(C)** such entity asserts a right of subrogation to the rights of such creditor under section 509 of this title.
>
> **(2)** A claim for reimbursement or contribution of such an entity that becomes fixed after the commencement of the case shall be determined, and shall be allowed under subsection (a), (b), or (c) of this section, or disallowed under subsection (d) of this section, the same as if such claim had become fixed before the date of the filing of the petition.

(f) In an involuntary case, a claim arising in the ordinary course of the debtor's business or financial affairs after the commencement of the case but before the earlier of the appointment of a trustee and the order for relief shall be determined as of the date such claim arises, and shall be allowed under subsection (a), (b), or (c) of this section or disallowed under subsection (d) or (e) of this section, the same as if such claim had arisen before the date of the filing of the petition.

> **(g)** **(1)** A claim arising from the rejection, under section 365 of this title or under a plan under chapter 9, 11, 12, or 13 of this title, of an executory contract or unexpired lease of the debtor that has not been assumed shall be determined, and shall be allowed under subsection (a), (b), or (c) of this section or disallowed under subsection (d) or (e) of this section, the same as if such claim had arisen before the date of the filing of the petition.
>
> **(2)** A claim for damages calculated in accordance with section 562 shall be allowed under subsection (a), (b) or (c) or disallowed under subsection (d) or (e) as if such claim had arisen before the date of the filing of the petition.

(h) A claim arising from the recovery of property under section 522, 550, or 553 of this title shall be determined, and shall be allowed under subsection (a), (b), or (c) of this section, or disallowed under subsection (d) or (e) of this section, the same as if such claim had arisen before the date of the filing of the petition.

(i) A claim that does not arise until after the commencement of the case for a tax entitled to priority under section 507 (a)(8) of this title shall be determined, and shall be allowed under subsection (a), (b), or (c) of this section, or disallowed under subsection (d) or (e) of this section, the same as if such claim had arisen before the date of the filing of the petition.

(j) A claim that has been allowed or disallowed may be reconsidered for cause. A reconsidered claim may be allowed or disallowed according to the equities of the case. Reconsideration of a claim under this subsection does not affect the validity of any payment or transfer from the estate made to a holder of an allowed claim on account of such allowed claim that is not reconsidered, but if a reconsidered claim is allowed and is of the same class as such holder's claim, such holder may not receive any additional payment or transfer from the estate on account of such holder's allowed claim until the holder of such reconsidered and allowed claim receives payment on account of such claim proportionate in value to that already received by such other holder. This subsection does not alter or modify the trustee's right to recover from a creditor any excess payment or transfer made to such creditor.

(k) **(1)** The court, on the motion of the debtor and after a hearing, may reduce a claim filed under this section based in whole on an unsecured consumer debt by not more than 20 percent of the claim, if —

(A) the claim was filed by a creditor who unreasonably refused to negotiate a reasonable alternative repayment schedule proposed on behalf of the debtor by an approved nonprofit budget and credit counseling agency described in section 111;

(B) the offer of the debtor under subparagraph (A) —

(i) was made at least 60 days before the date of the filing of the petition; and

(ii) provided for payment of at least 60 percent of the amount of the debt over a period not to exceed the repayment period of the loan, or a reasonable extension thereof; and

(C) no part of the debt under the alternative repayment schedule is nondischargeable.

(2) The debtor shall have the burden of proving, by clear and convincing evidence, that —

(A) the creditor unreasonably refused to consider the debtor's proposal; and

(B) the proposed alternative repayment schedule was made prior to expiration of the 60-day period specified in paragraph (1)(B)(i).

§ 503 Allowance of Administrative Expenses.

(a) An entity may timely file a request for payment of an administrative expense, or may tardily file such request if permitted by the court for cause.

(b) After notice and a hearing, there shall be allowed administrative expenses, other than claims allowed under section 502(f) of this title, including —

(1)   **(A)** the actual, necessary costs and expenses of preserving the estate including —

(i) wages, salaries, and commissions for services rendered after the commencement of the case; and

(ii) wages and benefits awarded pursuant to a judicial proceeding or a proceeding of the National Labor Relations Board as back pay attributable to any period of time occurring after commencement of the case under this title, as a result of a violation of Federal or State law by the debtor, without regard to the time of the occurrence of unlawful conduct on which such award is based or to whether any services were rendered, if the court determines that payment of wages and benefits by reason of the operation of this clause will not substantially increase the probability of layoff or termination of current employees, or of nonpayment of domestic support obligations, during the case under this title;

(B) any tax —

(i) incurred by the estate, whether secured or unsecured, including property taxes for which liability is in rem, in personam, or both, except a tax of a kind specified in section 507(a)(8) of this title; or

(ii) attributable to an excessive allowance of a tentative carryback adjustment that the estate received, whether the taxable year to which such adjustment relates ended before or after the commencement of the case;

(C) any fine, penalty, or reduction in credit relating to a tax of a kind specified in subparagraph (B) of this paragraph; and

(D) notwithstanding the requirements of subsection (a), a governmental unit shall not be required to file a request for the payment of an expense described in subparagraph (B) or (C), as a condition of its being an allowed administrative expense;

(2) compensation and reimbursement awarded under section 330(a) of this title;

(3) the actual, necessary expenses, other than compensation and reimbursement specified in paragraph (4) of this subsection, incurred by —

(A) a creditor that files a petition under section 303 of this title;

(B) a creditor that recovers, after the court's approval, for the benefit of the estate any property transferred or concealed by the debtor;

(C) a creditor in connection with the prosecution of a criminal offense relating to the case or to the business or property of the debtor;

(D) a creditor, an indenture trustee, an equity security holder, or a committee representing creditors or equity security holders other than a committee appointed under section 1102 of this title, in making a substantial contribution in a case under chapter 9 or 11 of this title;

(E) a custodian superseded under section 543 of this title, and compensation for the services of such custodian; or

(F) a member of a committee appointed under section 1102 of this title, if such expenses are incurred in the performance of the duties of such committee;

(4) reasonable compensation for professional services rendered by an attorney or an accountant of an entity whose expense is allowable under subparagraph (A), (B), (C), (D), or (E) of paragraph (3) of this subsection, based on the time, the nature, the extent, and the value of such services, and the cost of comparable services other than in a case under this title, and reimbursement for actual, necessary expenses incurred by such attorney or accountant;

(5) reasonable compensation for services rendered by an indenture trustee in making a substantial contribution in a case under chapter 9 or 11 of this title, based on the time, the nature, the extent, and the value of such services, and the cost of comparable services other than in a case under this title;

(6) the fees and mileage payable under chapter 119 of title 28;

(7) with respect to a nonresidential real property lease previously assumed under section 365, and subsequently rejected, a sum equal to all monetary obligations due, excluding those arising from or relating to a failure to operate or a penalty provision, for the period of 2 years following the later of the rejection date or the date of actual turnover of the premises, without reduction or setoff for any reason whatsoever except for sums actually received or to be received from an entity other than the debtor, and the claim for remaining sums due for the balance of the term of the lease shall be a claim under section 502(b)(6);

(8) the actual, necessary costs and expenses of closing a health care business incurred by a trustee or by a Federal agency (as defined in section 551(1) of title 5) or a department or agency of a State or political subdivision thereof, including any cost or incurred

—

(A) in disposing of patient records in accordance with section 351; or

(B) in connection with transferring patients from the health care business that is in the process of being closed to another health care business; and

(9) the value of any goods received by the debtor within 20 days before the date of commencement of a case under this title in which the goods have been sold to the debtor in the ordinary course of such debtor's business.

(c) Notwithstanding subsection (b), there shall neither be allowed, nor paid —

(1) a transfer made to, or an obligation incurred for the benefit of, an insider of the debtor for the purpose of inducing such person to remain with the debtor's business, absent a finding by the court based on evidence in the record that —

(A) the transfer or obligation is essential to retention of the person because the individual has a bona fide job offer from another business at the same or greater rate of compensation;

(B) the services provided by the person are essential to the survival of the business; and

(C) either —

(i) the amount of the transfer made to, or obligation incurred for the benefit of, the person is not greater than an amount equal to 10 times the amount of the mean transfer or obligation of a similar kind given to nonmanagement employees for any purpose during the calendar year in which the transfer is made or the obligation is incurred; or

(ii) if no such similar transfers were made to, or obligations were incurred for the benefit of, such nonmanagement employees during such calendar year, the amount of the transfer or obligation is not greater than an amount equal to 25 percent of the amount of any similar transfer or obligation made to or incurred for the benefit of such insider for any purpose during the calendar year before the year in which such transfer is made or obligation is incurred;

(2) a severance payment to an insider of the debtor, unless —

(A) the payment is part of a program that is generally applicable to all full-time employees; and

(B) the amount of the payment is not greater than 10 times the amount of the mean severance pay given to nonmanagement employees during the calendar year in which the payment is made; or

(3) other transfers or obligations that are outside the ordinary course of business and not justified by the facts and circumstances of the case, including transfers made to, or obligations incurred for the benefit of, officers, managers, or consultants hired after the date of the filing of the petition.

§ 506   Determination of secured status

(a)   (1) An allowed claim of a creditor secured by a lien on property in which the estate has an interest, or that is subject to setoff under section 553 of this title, is a secured claim to the extent of the value of such creditor's interest in the estate's interest in such property, or to the extent of the amount subject to setoff, as the case may be, and is an unsecured claim to the extent that the value of such creditor's interest or the amount so subject to setoff is less than the amount of such allowed claim. Such value shall be determined in light of the purpose of the valuation and of the proposed disposition or use of such property, and in conjunction with any hearing on such disposition or use or on a plan affecting such creditor's interest.

(2)   If the debtor is an individual in a case under Chapter 7 or 13, such value with respect to personal property securing an allowed claim shall be determined based on the replacement value of such property as of the date of the filing of the petition without deduction for costs of sale or marketing. With respect to property acquired for personal, family, or household purposes, replacement value shall mean the price a retail merchant would charge for property of that kind considering the age and condition of the property at the time value determined.

(b) To the extent that an allowed secured claim is secured by property the value of which, after any recovery under subsection (c) of this section, is greater than the amount of such claim, there shall be allowed to the holder of such claim, interest on such claim, and any reasonable fees, costs, or charges provided for under the agreement or State statute under which such claim arose.

(c) The trustee may recover from property securing an allowed secured claim the reasonable, necessary costs and expenses of preserving, or disposing of, such property to the extent of any benefit to the holder of such claim, including the payment of all ad valorem property taxes with respect to the property.

(d) To the extent that a lien secures a claim against the debtor that is not an allowed secured claim, such lien is void, unless—

(1) such claim was disallowed only under section 502 (b)(5) or 502 (e) of this title; or

(2) such claim is not an allowed secured claim due only to the failure of any entity to file a proof of such claim under section 501 of this title.

§ 507   Priorities

(a) The following expenses and claims have priority in the following order:

(1) First:

(A)   Allowed   unsecured   claims   for   domestic   support obligations that, as of the date of the filing of the petition in a case under this title, are owed to or recoverable by a spouse, former spouse, or child of the debtor, or such child's parent, legal guardian, or responsible relative, without regard to whether the claim is filed by such person or is filed by a governmental unit on behalf of such person, on the condition that funds received under this paragraph by a governmental unit under this title after the date of the filing of the petition shall be applied and distributed in accordance with applicable nonbankruptcy law.

(B) Subject to claims under subparagraph (A), allowed unsecured claims for domestic support obligations that, as of the date of the filing of the petition, are assigned by a spouse, former spouse, child of the debtor, or such child's parent, legal guardian, or responsible relative to a governmental unit (unless such obligation is assigned voluntarily by the spouse, former spouse, child, parent, legal guardian, or responsible relative of the child for the purpose of collecting the debt) or are owed directly to or recoverable by a governmental unit under applicable nonbankruptcy law, on the condition that funds received under this paragraph by a governmental unit under this title after the date of the filing of the petition be applied and distributed in accordance with applicable nonbankruptcy law.

(C) If a trustee is appointed or elected under section 701, 702, 703, 1104, 1202, or 1302, the administrative expenses of the trustee allowed under paragraphs (1)(A), (2), and (6) of section 503(b) shall be paid before payment of claims under subparagraphs (A) and (B), to the extent that the trustee administers assets that are otherwise available for the payment of such claims.

(2) Second, administrative expenses allowed under section 503 (b) of this title, and any fees and charges assessed against the estate under chapter 123 of title 28.

(3) Third, unsecured claims allowed under section 502 (f) of this title.

(4) Fourth, allowed unsecured claims, but only to the extent of $4,000 for each individual or corporation, as the case may be, earned within 90 days before the date of the filing of the petition or the date of the cessation of the debtor's business, whichever occurs first, for—

(A) wages, salaries, or commissions, including vacation, severance, and sick leave pay earned by an individual; or

(B) sales commissions earned by an individual or by a corporation with only 1 employee, acting as an independent contractor in the sale of goods or services for the debtor in the ordinary course of the debtor's business if, and only if, during the 12 months preceding that date, at least 75 percent of the amount that the individual or corporation earned by acting as an independent contractor in the sale of goods or services was earned from the debtor;

(5) Fifth, allowed unsecured claims for contributions to an employee benefit plan—

(A) arising from services rendered within 180 days before the date of the filing of the petition or the date of the cessation of the debtor's business, whichever occurs first; but only

(B) for each such plan, to the extent of—

(i) the number of employees covered by each such plan multiplied by $4,000; less

(ii) the aggregate amount paid to such employees under paragraph (3) of this subsection, plus the aggregate amount paid by the estate on behalf of such employees to any other employee benefit plan.

(6) Sixth, allowed unsecured claims of persons—

(A) engaged in the production or raising of grain, as defined in section 557 (b) of this title, against a debtor who owns or operates a grain storage facility, as defined in section 557 (b) of this title, for grain or the proceeds of grain, or

(B) engaged as a United States fisherman against a debtor who has acquired fish or fish produce from a fisherman through a sale or conversion, and who is engaged in operating a fish produce storage or processing facility—

but only to the extent of $4,000 for each such individual.

(7) Seventh, allowed unsecured claims of individuals, to the extent of $1,800 for each such individual, arising from the deposit, before the commencement of the case, of money in connection with the purchase, lease, or rental of property, or the purchase of services, for the personal, family, or household use of such individuals, that were not delivered or provided.

(8) Eighth, allowed unsecured claims of governmental units, only to the extent that such claims are for—

(A) a tax on or measured by income or gross receipts for a taxable year ending on or before the date of the filing of the petition—

(i) for which a return, if required, is last due, including extensions, after three years before the date of the filing of the petition;

(ii) assessed within 240 days before the date pf the filing of the petition, exclusive of –

(I) Any time during which an offer in compromise

139

with respect to that tax was pending or in effect during the 240-day period, plus 30 days; and

(II) any time during which a stay of proceedings against collections was in effect in a prior case under which title during that 240-day period, plus 90 days.

(iii) other than a tax of a kind specified in section 523 (a)(1)(B) or 523 (a)(1)(C) of this title, not assessed before, but assessable, under applicable law or by agreement, after, the commencement of the case;

(B) a property tax incurred before the commencement of the case and last payable without penalty after one year before the date of the filing of the petition;

(C) a tax required to be collected or withheld and for which the debtor is liable in whatever capacity;

(D) an employment tax on a wage, salary, or commission of a kind specified in paragraph (3) of this subsection earned from the debtor before the date of the filing of the petition, whether or not actually paid before such date, for which a return is last due, under applicable law or under any extension, after three years before the date of the filing of the petition;

(E) an excise tax on—

(i) a transaction occurring before the date of the filing of the petition for which a return, if required, is last due, under applicable law or under any extension, after three years before the date of the filing of the petition; or

(ii) if a return is not required, a transaction occurring during the three years immediately preceding the date of the filing of the petition;

(F) a customs duty arising out of the importation of merchandise—

(i) entered for consumption within one year before the date of the filing of the petition;

(ii) covered by an entry liquidated or reliquidated within one year before the date of the filing of the petition; or

(iii) entered for consumption within four years before the date of the filing of the petition but unliquidated on such date, if the Secretary of the Treasury certifies that failure to liquidate such entry was due to an investigation pending on such date into assessment of antidumping or countervailing duties or fraud, or if information needed for the proper appraisement or classification of such merchandise was not available to the appropriate customs officer before such date; or

(G) a penalty related to a claim of a kind specified in this paragraph and in compensation for actual pecuniary loss. An otherwise applicable time period specified in this paragraph shall be suspended for any period during which a governmental unit is prohibited under applicable nonbankruptcy law from collecting a tax as a result of a request by the debtor for a hearing and an appeal of any collection action taken or proposed against the debtor, plus 90 days; plus any time during which the stay of proceedings was in effect in a prior case under this title or during which a collection was precluded by the existence of 1 or more confirmed plans under this title, plus 90 days.

(9) Ninth, allowed unsecured claims based upon any commitment by the debtor to a Federal depository institutions regulatory agency (or predecessor to such agency) to maintain the capital of an insured depository institution.

(10) Tenth, allowed claims for death or personal injury resulting from the operation of a motor vehicle or vessel if such operation was unlawful because the debtor was intoxicated, using alcohol, a drug, or another substance.

(b) If the trustee, under section 362, 363, or 364 of this title, provides adequate protection of the interest of a holder of a claim secured by a lien on property of the debtor and if, notwithstanding such protection, such creditor has a claim allowable under subsection (a)(1) of this section arising from the stay of action against such property under section 362 of this title, from the use, sale, or lease of such property under section 363 of this title, or from the granting of a lien under section 364 (d) of this title, then such creditor's claim under such subsection shall have priority over every other claim allowable under such subsection.

(c) For the purpose of subsection (a) of this section, a claim of a governmental unit arising from an erroneous refund or credit of a tax has the same priority as a claim for the tax to which such refund or credit relates.

(d) An entity that is subrogated to the rights of a holder of a claim of a kind specified in subsection (a)(1), (a)(4), (a)(5), (a)(6), (a)(7), (a)(8), or (a)(9) of this section is not subrogated to the right of the holder of such claim to priority under such subsection.

§ 524 Effect of discharge

(a) A discharge in a case under this title—

(1) voids any judgment at any time obtained, to the extent that such judgment is a determination of the personal liability of the debtor with respect to any debt discharged under section 727, 944, 1141, 1228, or 1328 of this title, whether or not discharge of such debt is waived;

(2) operates as an injunction against the commencement or continuation of an action, the employment of process, or an act, to collect, recover or offset any such debt as a personal liability of

the debtor, whether or not discharge of such debt is waived; and
(3) operates as an injunction against the commencement or continuation of an action, the employment of process, or an act, to collect or recover from, or offset against, property of the debtor of the kind specified in section 541 (a)(2) of this title that is acquired after the commencement of the case, on account of any allowable community claim, except a community claim that is excepted from discharge under section 523, 1228 (a)(1), or 1328 (a)(1) of this title, or that would be so excepted, determined in accordance with the provisions of sections 523 (c) and 523 (d) of this title, in a case concerning the debtor's spouse commenced on the date of the filing of the petition in the case concerning the debtor, whether or not discharge of the debt based on such community claim is waived. . .

(g) (1)

(A) After notice and hearing, a court that enters an order confirming a Plan of Reorganization under chapter 11 may issue, in connection with such order, an injunction in accordance with this subsection to supplement the injunctive effect of a discharge under this section.

(B) An injunction may be issued under subparagraph (A) to enjoin entities from taking legal action for the purpose of directly or indirectly collecting, recovering, or receiving payment or recovery with respect to any claim or demand that, under a Plan of Reorganization, is to be paid in whole or in part by a trust described in paragraph (2)(B)(i), except such legal actions as are expressly allowed by the injunction, the confirmation order, or the Plan of Reorganization.

(2)

(A) Subject to subsection (h), if the requirements of subparagraph (B) are met at the time an injunction described in paragraph (1) is entered, then after entry of such injunction, any proceeding that involves the validity, application, construction, or modification of such injunction, or of this subsection with respect to such injunction, may be commenced only in the district court in which such injunction was entered, and such court shall have exclusive jurisdiction over any such proceeding without regard to the amount in controversy.

(B) The requirements of this subparagraph are that—

(i) the injunction is to be implemented in connection with a trust that, pursuant to the Plan of Reorganization—

(I) is to assume the liabilities of a debtor which at the time of entry of the order for relief has been named as a defendant in personal injury, wrongful death, or property-damage actions seeking recovery for damages allegedly caused by the presence of, or exposure to, asbestos or asbestos-containing products;

(II) is to be funded in whole or in part by the securities of 1 or more debtors involved in such plan and by the obligation of such debtor or debtors to make future payments, including dividends;

(III) is to own, or by the exercise of rights granted under such plan would be entitled to own if specified contingencies occur, a majority of the voting shares of—

    (aa) each such debtor;

    (bb) the parent corporation of each such debtor; or

    (cc) a subsidiary of each such debtor that is also a debtor; and

(IV) is to use its assets or income to pay claims and demands; and

(ii) subject to subsection (h), the court determines that—

(I) the debtor is likely to be subject to substantial future demands for payment arising out of the same or similar conduct or events that gave rise to the claims that are addressed by the injunction;

(II) the actual amounts, numbers, and timing of such future demands cannot be determined;

(III) pursuit of such demands outside the procedures prescribed by such plan is likely to threaten the plan's purpose to deal equitably with claims and future demands;

(IV) as part of the process of seeking confirmation of such plan—

    (aa) the terms of the injunction proposed to be issued under paragraph (1)(A), including any provisions barring actions against third parties pursuant to paragraph (4)(A), are set out in such plan and in any disclosure statement supporting the plan; and

    (bb) a separate class or classes of the claimants whose claims are to be addressed by a trust described in clause (i) is established and votes, by at least 75 percent of those voting, in favor of the plan; and

(V) subject to subsection (h), pursuant to court orders or otherwise, the trust will operate through mechanisms such as structured, periodic, or supplemental payments, pro rata distributions, matrices, or periodic review of estimates of the numbers and values of present claims and future demands, or other comparable mechanisms, that provide reasonable assurance that the trust will value, and be in a financial position to pay, present claims and future demands that involve similar claims in substantially the same manner.

(3)

(A) If the requirements of paragraph (2)(B) are met and the order confirming the Plan of Reorganization was issued or affirmed by the district court that has jurisdiction over the reorganization case, then after the time for appeal of the order that issues or affirms the plan—

> **(i)** the injunction shall be valid and enforceable and may not be revoked or modified by any court except through appeal in accordance with paragraph (6);
>
> **(ii)** no entity that pursuant to such plan or thereafter becomes a direct or indirect transferee of, or successor to any assets of, a debtor or trust that is the subject of the injunction shall be liable with respect to any claim or demand made against such entity by reason of its becoming such a transferee or successor; and
>
> **(iii)** no entity that pursuant to such plan or thereafter makes a loan to such a debtor or trust or to such a successor or transferee shall, by reason of making the loan, be liable with respect to any claim or demand made against such entity, nor shall any pledge of assets made in connection with such a loan be upset or impaired for that reason;

(B) Subparagraph (A) shall not be construed to—

> **(i)** imply that an entity described in subparagraph (A)(ii) or (iii) would, if this paragraph were not applicable, necessarily be liable to any entity by reason of any of the acts described in subparagraph (A);
>
> **(ii)** relieve any such entity of the duty to comply with, or of liability under, any Federal or State law regarding the making of a fraudulent conveyance in a transaction described in subparagraph (A)(ii) or (iii); or
>
> **(iii)** relieve a debtor of the debtor's obligation to comply with the terms of the Plan of Reorganization, or affect the power of the court to exercise its authority under sections 1141 and 1142 to compel the debtor to do so.

(4)

(A)

> **(i)** Subject to subparagraph (B), an injunction

described in paragraph (1) shall be valid and enforceable against all entities that it addresses.

(ii) Notwithstanding the provisions of section 524 (e), such an injunction may bar any action directed against a third party who is identifiable from the terms of such injunction (by name or as part of an identifiable group) and is alleged to be directly or indirectly liable for the conduct of, claims against, or demands on the debtor to the extent such alleged liability of such third party arises by reason of—

(I) the third party's ownership of a financial interest in the debtor, a past or present affiliate of the debtor, or a predecessor in interest of the debtor;

(II) the third party's involvement in the management of the debtor or a predecessor in interest of the debtor, or service as an officer, director or employee of the debtor or a related party;

(III) the third party's provision of insurance to the debtor or a related party; or

(IV) the third party's involvement in a transaction changing the corporate structure, or in a loan or other financial transaction affecting the financial condition, of the debtor or a related party, including but not limited to—

> **(aa)** involvement in providing financing (debt or equity), or advice to an entity involved in such a transaction; or
>
> **(bb)** acquiring or selling a financial interest in an entity as part of such a transaction.

(iii) As used in this subparagraph, the term "related party" means—

(I) a past or present affiliate of the debtor;

(II) a predecessor in interest of the debtor; or

(III) any entity that owned a financial interest in—

> **(aa)** the debtor;
>
> **(bb)** a past or present affiliate of the debtor; or
>
> **(cc)** a predecessor in interest of the debtor.

(B) Subject to subsection (h), if, under a Plan of Reorganization, a kind of demand described in such plan is to be paid in whole or in part by a trust described in paragraph (2)(B)(i) in connection with which an injunction described in paragraph (1) is to be implemented, then such injunction shall be valid and enforceable with respect to a demand of such kind made, after such plan is confirmed, against the debtor or debtors involved, or against a third party described in subparagraph (A)(ii), if—

> **(i)** as part of the proceedings leading to issuance of such injunction, the court appoints a legal

representative for the purpose of protecting the rights of persons that might subsequently assert demands of such kind, and

(ii) the court determines, before entering the order confirming such plan, that identifying such debtor or debtors, or such third party (by name or as part of an identifiable group), in such injunction with respect to such demands for purposes of this subparagraph is fair and equitable with respect to the persons that might subsequently assert such demands, in light of the benefits provided, or to be provided, to such trust on behalf of such debtor or debtors or such third party.

(5) In this subsection, the term "demand" means a demand for payment, present or future, that—

(A) was not a claim during the proceedings leading to the confirmation of a Plan of Reorganization;

(B) arises out of the same or similar conduct or events that gave rise to the claims addressed by the injunction issued under paragraph (1); and

(C) pursuant to the plan, is to be paid by a trust described in paragraph (2)(B)(i).

(6) Paragraph (3)(A)(i) does not bar an action taken by or at the direction of an appellate court on appeal of an injunction issued under paragraph (1) or of the order of confirmation that relates to the injunction.

(7) This subsection does not affect the operation of section 1144 or the power of the district court to refer a proceeding under section 157 of title 28 or any reference of a proceeding made prior to the date of the enactment of this subsection.

(h) Application to Existing Injunctions.— For purposes of subsection (g)—

(1) subject to paragraph (2), if an injunction of the kind described in subsection (g)(1)(B) was issued before the date of the enactment of this Act, as part of a Plan of Reorganization confirmed by an order entered before such date, then the injunction shall be considered to meet the requirements of subsection (g)(2)(B) for purposes of subsection (g)(2)(A), and to satisfy subsection (g)(4)(A)(ii), if—

(A) the court determined at the time the plan was confirmed that the plan was fair and equitable in accordance with the requirements of section 1129 (b);

(B) as part of the proceedings leading to issuance of such injunction and confirmation of such plan, the court had appointed a legal representative for the purpose of protecting the rights of persons that might subsequently assert demands described in subsection (g)(4)(B) with respect to such plan; and

(C) such legal representative did not object to confirmation of such plan or issuance of such injunction; and

(2) for purposes of paragraph (1), if a trust described in subsection (g)(2)(B)(i) is subject to a court order on the date of the enactment of this Act staying such trust from settling or paying further claims—

> **(A)** the requirements of subsection (g)(2)(B)(ii)(V) shall not apply with respect to such trust until such stay is lifted or dissolved; and
>
> **(B)** if such trust meets such requirements on the date such stay is lifted or dissolved, such trust shall be considered to have met such requirements continuously from the date of the enactment of this Act.

>> **(i)** The willful failure of a creditor to credit payments received under a plan confirmed under this title, unless the order confirming the plan is revoked, the plan is in default, or the creditor has not received payments required to be made under the plan in the manner required by the plan (including crediting the amounts required under the plan), shall constitute a violation of an injunction under subsection (a)(2) if the act of the creditor to collect and failure to credit payments in the manner required by the plan caused material injury to the debtor.
>>
>> **(j)** Subsection (a)(2) does not operate as an injunction against an act by a creditor that is the holder of a secured claim, if —

(1) such creditor retains a security interest in real property that is the principal residence of the debtor;

(2) such act is in the ordinary course of business between the creditor and the debtor; and **(3)** such act is limited to seeking or obtaining periodic payments associated with a valid security interest in lieu of pursuit of in rem relief to enforce the lien.

(k) **(1)** The disclosures required under subsection (c)(2) shall consist of the disclosure statement described in paragraph (3), completed as required in that paragraph, together with the agreement specified in subsection (c), statement, declaration, motion and order described, respectively, in paragraphs (4) through (8), and shall be the only disclosures required in connection with entering into such agreement.

(2) Disclosures made under paragraph (1) shall be made clearly and conspicuously and in writing. The terms "Amount Reaffirmed" and "Annual Percentage Rate" shall be disclosed more conspicuously than other terms, data or information provided in connection with this disclosure, except that the phrases "Before agreeing to reaffirm a debt, review these important disclosures" and "Summary of Reaffirmation Agreement" may be equally conspicuous. Disclosures may be made in a different order and may use terminology different from that set forth in paragraphs (2) through (8), except that the terms "Amount Reaffirmed" and "Annual Percentage Rate" must be used where indicated.

(3) The disclosure statement required under this paragraph shall consist of the following:

(A) The statement: "Part A: Before agreeing to reaffirm a debt, review these important disclosures:";

(B) Under the heading "Summary of Reaffirmation Agreement", the statement: "This Summary is made pursuant to the requirements of the Bankruptcy Code";

(C) The "Amount Reaffirmed", using that term, which shall be —

(i) the total amount of debt that the debtor agrees to reaffirm by entering into an agreement of the kind specified in subsection (c), and

(ii) the total of any fees and costs accrued as of the date of the disclosure statement, related to such total amount.

(D) In conjunction with the disclosure of the "Amount Reaffirmed", the statements —

(i) "The amount of debt you have agreed to reaffirm"; and **(ii)** "Your credit agreement may obligate you to pay additional amounts which may come due after the date of this disclosure. Consult your credit agreement.".

(E) The "Annual Percentage Rate", using that term, which shall be disclosed as —

(i) if, at the time the petition is filed, the debt is an extension of credit under an open end credit plan, as the terms "credit" and "open end credit plan" are defined in section 103 of the Truth in Lending Act, then —

(I) the annual percentage rate determined under paragraphs (5) and (6) of section 127(b) of the Truth in Lending Act, as applicable, as disclosed to the debtor in the most recent periodic statement prior to entering into an agreement of the kind specified in subsection (c) or, if no such periodic statement has been given to the debtor during the prior 6 months, the annual percentage rate as it would have been so disclosed at the time the disclosure statement is given to the debtor, or to the extent this annual percentage rate is not readily available or not applicable, then

(II) the simple interest rate applicable to the amount reaffirmed as of the date the disclosure statement is given to the debtor, or if different simple interest rates apply to different balances, the simple interest rate applicable to each such balance, identifying the amount of each such balance included in the amount reaffirmed, or

(III) if the entity making the disclosure elects, to disclose the annual percentage rate under subclause (I) and the simple interest rate under subclause (II); or

(ii) if, at the time the petition is filed, the debt is an extension of credit other than under an open end credit plan, as the terms "credit" and "open end credit plan" are defined in section 103 of the Truth in Lending Act, then —

(I) the annual percentage rate under section 128(a)(4) of the Truth in Lending Act, as disclosed to the debtor in the most recent disclosure statement given to the debtor prior to the entering into an agreement of the kind specified in subsection (c) with respect to the debt, or, if no such disclosure statement was given to the debtor, the annual percentage rate as it would have been so disclosed at the time the disclosure statement is given to the debtor, or to the extent this annual percentage rate is not readily available or not applicable, then

(II) the simple interest rate applicable to the amount reaffirmed as of the date the disclosure statement is given to the debtor, or if different simple interest rates apply to different balances, the simple interest rate applicable to each such balance, identifying the amount of such balance included in the amount reaffirmed, or

(III) if the entity making the disclosure elects, to disclose the annual percentage rate under (I) and the simple interest rate under (II).

(F) If the underlying debt transaction was disclosed as a variable rate transaction on the most recent disclosure given under the Truth in Lending Act, by stating "The interest rate on your loan may be a variable interest rate which changes from time to time, so that the annual percentage rate disclosed here may be higher or lower.".

(G) If the debt is secured by a security interest which has not been waived in whole or in part or determined to be void by a final order of the court at the time of the disclosure, by disclosing that a security interest or lien in goods or property is asserted over some or all of the debts the debtor is reaffirming and listing the items and their original purchase price that are subject to the asserted security interest, or if not a purchase-money security interest then listing by items or types and the original amount of the loan.

(H) At the election of the creditor, a statement of the repayment schedule using 1 or a combination of the following —

> **(i)** by making the statement: "Your first payment in the amount of $___ is due on ___ but the future payment amount may be different. Consult your reaffirmation agreement or credit agreement, as applicable.", and stating the amount of the first payment and the due date of that payment in the places provided;
>
> **(ii)** by making the statement: "Your payment schedule will be:", and describing the repayment schedule with the number, amount, and due dates or period of payments scheduled to repay the debts reaffirmed to the extent then known by the disclosing party; or
>
> **(iii)** by describing the debtor's repayment obligations with reasonable specificity to the extent then known by the disclosing party.

(I) The following statement: "Note: When this disclosure refers to what a creditor `may' do, it does not use the word `may' to give the creditor specific permission. The word `may' is used to tell you what might occur if the law permits the creditor to take the action. If you have questions about your reaffirming a debt or what the law requires, consult with the attorney who helped you negotiate this agreement reaffirming a debt. If you don't have an attorney helping you, the judge will explain the effect of your reaffirming a debt when the hearing on the reaffirmation agreement is held.".

(J)(i) The following additional statements: "Reaffirming a debt is a serious financial decision. The law requires you to take certain steps to make sure the decision is in your best interest. If these steps are not completed, the reaffirmation agreement is not effective, even though you have signed it.

"1. Read the disclosures in this Part A carefully. Consider the decision to reaffirm carefully. Then, if you want to reaffirm, sign the reaffirmation agreement in Part B (or you may use a separate agreement you and your creditor agree on).

"2. Complete and sign Part D and be sure you can afford to make the payments you are agreeing to make and have received a copy of the disclosure statement and a completed and signed reaffirmation agreement.

"3. If you were represented by an attorney during the negotiation of your reaffirmation agreement, the attorney must have signed the certification in Part C.

"4. If you were not represented by an attorney during the negotiation of your reaffirmation agreement, you must have completed and signed Part E.

"5. The original of this disclosure must be filed with the court by you or your creditor. If a separate reaffirmation agreement (other than the one in Part B) has been signed, it must be attached.

"6. If you were represented by an attorney during the negotiation of your reaffirmation agreement, your reaffirmation agreement becomes effective upon filing with the court unless the reaffirmation is presumed to be an undue hardship as explained in Part D.

"7. If you were not represented by an attorney during the negotiation of your reaffirmation agreement, it will not be effective unless the court approves it. The court will notify you of the hearing on your reaffirmation agreement. You must attend this hearing in Bankruptcy Court where the judge will review your reaffirmation agreement. The Bankruptcy Court must approve your reaffirmation agreement as consistent with your best interests, except that no court approval is required if your reaffirmation agreement is for a consumer debt secured by a mortgage, deed of trust, security deed, or other lien on your real property, like your home.

"Your right to rescind (cancel) your reaffirmation agreement.

You may rescind (cancel) your reaffirmation agreement at any time before the Bankruptcy Court enters a discharge order, or before the expiration of the 60-day period that begins on the date your reaffirmation agreement is filed with the court, whichever occurs later. To rescind (cancel) your reaffirmation agreement, you must notify the creditor that your reaffirmation agreement is rescinded (or canceled).

"What are your obligations if you reaffirm the debt? A reaffirmed debt remains your personal legal obligation. It is not discharged in your bankruptcy case. That means that if you default on your reaffirmed debt after your bankruptcy case is over, your creditor may be able to take your property or your wages. Otherwise, your obligations will be determined by the reaffirmation agreement which may have changed the terms of the original agreement. For example, if you are reaffirming an open end credit agreement, the creditor may be permitted by that agreement or applicable law to change the terms of that agreement in the future under certain conditions.

"Are you required to enter into a reaffirmation agreement by any law? No, you are not required to reaffirm a debt by any law. Only agree to reaffirm a debt if it is in your best interest. Be sure you can afford the payments you agree to make.

"What if your creditor has a security interest or lien? Your bankruptcy discharge does not eliminate any lien on your property. A `lien' is often referred to as a security interest, deed of trust, mortgage or security deed. Even if you do not reaffirm and your personal liability on the debt is discharged,

because of the lien your creditor may still have the right to take the security property if you do not pay the debt or default on it. If the lien is on an item of personal property that is exempt under your State's law or that the trustee has abandoned, you may be able to redeem the item rather than reaffirm the debt. To redeem, you make a single payment to the creditor equal to the current value of the security property, as agreed by the parties or determined by the court."

(ii) In the case of a reaffirmation under subsection (m)(2), numbered paragraph 6 in the disclosures required by clause **(i)** of this subparagraph shall read as follows:

"6. If you were represented by an attorney during the negotiation of your reaffirmation agreement, your reaffirmation agreement becomes effective upon filing with the court.".

(4) The form of such agreement required under this paragraph shall consist of the following:

"Part B: Reaffirmation Agreement. I (we) agree to reaffirm the debts arising under the credit agreement described below.

"Brief description of credit agreement:

"Description of any changes to the credit agreement made as part of this reaffirmation agreement:

"Signature:　　　　　Date:

"Borrower:

"Co-borrower, if also reaffirming these debts:

"Accepted by creditor:

"Date of creditor acceptance:".

(5) The declaration shall consist of the following:

(A) The following certification:

"Part C: Certification by Debtor's Attorney (If Any).

"I hereby certify that (1) this agreement represents a fully informed and voluntary agreement by the debtor; (2) this agreement does not impose an undue hardship on the debtor or any dependent of the debtor; and (3) I have fully advised the debtor of the legal effect and consequences of this agreement and any default under this agreement.

"Signature of Debtor's Attorney:　　Date:".

(B) If a presumption of undue hardship has been established with respect to such agreement, such certification shall state that in the opinion of the attorney, the debtor is able to make the payment.

(C) In the case of a reaffirmation agreement under subsection (m)(2), subparagraph (B) is not applicable.

(6)　　**(A)** The statement in support of such agreement, which the debtor shall sign and date prior to filing with the court, shall consist of the following:

"Part D: Debtor's Statement in Support of Reaffirmation Agreement.

"1. I believe this reaffirmation agreement will not impose an undue hardship on my dependents or me. I can afford to make the payments on the reaffirmed debt because my monthly income (take home pay plus any other income received) is $___, and my actual current monthly expenses including monthly payments on post-bankruptcy debt

and other reaffirmation agreements total $___, leaving

$___ to make the required payments on this reaffirmed debt. I understand that if my income less my monthly expenses does not leave enough to make the payments, this reaffirmation agreement is presumed to be an undue hardship on me and must be reviewed by the court. However, this presumption may be overcome if I explain to the satisfaction of the court how I can afford to make the payments here: ___"

"2. I received a copy of the Reaffirmation Disclosure Statement in Part A and a completed and signed reaffirmation agreement."

(B) Where the debtor is represented by an attorney and is reaffirming a debt owed to a creditor defined in section 19(b)(1)(A)(iv) of the Federal Reserve Act, the statement of support of the reaffirmation agreement, which the debtor shall sign and date prior to filing with the court, shall consist of the following:

"I believe this reaffirmation agreement is in my financial interest. I can afford to make the payments on the reaffirmed debt. I received a copy of the Reaffirmation Disclosure Statement in Part A and a completed and signed reaffirmation agreement."

(7) The motion that may be used if approval of such agreement by the court is required in order for it to be effective, shall be signed and dated by the movant and shall consist of the following:

"Part E: Motion for Court Approval (To be completed only if the debtor is not represented by an attorney.). I (we), the debtor(s), affirm the following to be true and correct: "I am not represented by an attorney in connection with this reaffirmation agreement. "I believe this reaffirmation agreement is in my best interest based on the income and expenses I have disclosed in my Statement in Support of this reaffirmation agreement, and because (provide any additional relevant reasons the court should consider):

"Therefore, I ask the court for an order approving this reaffirmation agreement."

(8) The court order, which may be used to approve such agreement, shall consist of the following:

"Court Order: The court grants the debtor's motion and approves the reaffirmation agreement described above."

(l) Notwithstanding any other provision of this title the following shall apply:

(1) A creditor may accept payments from a debtor before and after the filing of an agreement of the kind specified in subsection (c) with the court.

(2) A creditor may accept payments from a debtor under such agreement that the creditor believes in good faith to be effective.

(3) The requirements of subsections (c)(2) and (k) shall be satisfied if disclosures required under those subsections are given in good faith.

(m)(1) Until 60 days after an agreement of the kind specified in subsection (c) is filed with the court (or such additional period as the court, after notice and a hearing and for cause, orders before the expiration of such period), it shall be presumed that such agreement is an undue hardship on the debtor if the debtor's monthly income less the debtor's monthly expenses as shown on the debtor's completed and signed statement in support of such agreement required under subsection (k)(6)(A) is less than the scheduled payments on the reaffirmed debt. This presumption shall be reviewed by the court. The presumption may be rebutted in writing by the debtor if the statement includes an explanation that identifies additional sources of funds to make the payments as agreed upon under the terms of such agreement. If the presumption is not rebutted to the satisfaction of the court, the court may disapprove such agreement. No agreement shall be disapproved without notice and a hearing to the debtor and creditor, and such hearing shall be concluded before the entry of the debtor's discharge.

(2) This subsection does not apply to reaffirmation agreements where the creditor is a credit union, as defined in section19 (b)(1)(A)(iv) of the Federal Reserve Act.

§ 541 Property of the estate

(a) The commencement of a case under section 301, 302, or 303 of this title creates an estate. Such estate is comprised of all the following property, wherever located and by whomever held:

(1) Except as provided in subsections (b) and (c)(2) of this section, all legal or equitable interests of the debtor in property as of the commencement of the case.

(2) All interests of the debtor and the debtor's spouse in community property as of the commencement of the case that is—

(A) under the sole, equal, or joint management and control of the debtor; or

(B) liable for an allowable claim against the debtor, or for both an allowable claim against the debtor and an allowable claim against the debtor's spouse, to the extent that such interest is so liable.

(3) Any interest in property that the trustee recovers under section 329 (b), 363 (n), 543, 550, 553, or 723 of this title.

(4) Any interest in property preserved for the benefit of or ordered transferred to the estate under section 510 (c) or 551 of this title.

(5) Any interest in property that would have been property of the estate if such interest had been an interest of the debtor on the date of the filing of the petition, and that the debtor acquires or becomes entitled to acquire within 180 days after such date—

(A) by bequest, devise, or inheritance;

(B) as a result of a property settlement agreement with the debtor's spouse, or of an interlocutory or final divorce decree; or

(C) as a beneficiary of a life insurance policy or of a death benefit plan.

(6) Proceeds, product, offspring, rents, or profits of or from property of the estate, except such as are earnings from services performed by an individual debtor after the commencement of the case.

(7) Any interest in property that the estate acquires after the commencement of the case.

(b) Property of the estate does not include—

(1) any power that the debtor may exercise solely for the benefit of an entity other than the debtor;

(2) any interest of the debtor as a lessee under a lease of nonresidential real property that has terminated at the expiration of the stated term of such lease before the commencement of the case under this title, and ceases to include any interest of the debtor as a lessee under a lease of nonresidential real property that has terminated at the expiration of the stated term of such lease during the case;

(3) any eligibility of the debtor to participate in programs authorized under the Higher Education Act of 1965 (20 U.S.C. 1001 et seq.; 42 U.S.C. 2751 et seq.), or any accreditation status or State licensure of the debtor as an educational institution;

(4) any interest of the debtor in liquid or gaseous hydrocarbons to the extent that—

(A)

(i) the debtor has transferred or has agreed to transfer such interest pursuant to a farm out agreement or any written agreement directly related to a farm out agreement; and

(ii) but for the operation of this paragraph, the estate could include the interest referred to in clause (i) only by virtue of section 365 or 544 (a)(3) of this title; or

(B)

(i) the debtor has transferred such interest pursuant to a written conveyance of a production payment to an entity that does not participate in the operation of the property from which such production payment is transferred; and

(ii) but for the operation of this paragraph, the estate could include the interest referred to in clause (i) only by virtue of section 365 or 542 of this title; or

(5) funds placed in an education individual retirement account as defined in section 530(b)(1) of the Internal Revenue Code of 1986) not later than 365 days before the date of the filing of the petition in a case under this title, but —

    (A) only if the designated beneficiary of such account was a child, stepchild, grandchild, or stepgrandchild of the debtor for the taxable year for which funds were placed in such account;

    (B) only to the extent that such funds —

        (i) are not pledged or promised to any entity in connection with any extension of credit; and

        (ii) are not excess contributions (as described in section 4973(e) of the Internal Revenue Code of 1986); and

    (C) in the case of funds placed in all such accounts having the same designated beneficiary not earlier than 720 days nor later than 365 days before such date, only so much of such funds as does not exceed $5,000;

(6) funds used to purchase a tuition credit or certificate or contributed to an account in accordance with section 529(b)(1)(A) of the Internal Revenue Code of 1986 under a qualified State tuition program (as defined in section 529(b)(1) of such Code) not later than 365 days before the date of the filing of the petition in a case under this title, but —

    (A) only if the designated beneficiary of the amounts paid or contributed to such tuition program was a child, stepchild, grandchild, or stepgrandchild of the debtor for the taxable year for which funds were paid or contributed;

    (B) with respect to the aggregate amount paid or contributed to such program having the same designated beneficiary, only so much of such amount as does not exceed the total contributions permitted under section 529(b)(7) of such Code with respect to such beneficiary, as adjusted beginning on the date of the filing of the petition in a case under this title by the annual increase or decrease (rounded to the nearest tenth of 1 percent) in the education expenditure category of the Consumer Price Index prepared by the Department of Labor; and

    (C) in the case of funds paid or contributed to such program having the same designated beneficiary not earlier than 720 days nor later than 365 days before such date, only so much of such funds as does not exceed $5,000;

(7) any amount —

    (A) withheld by an employer from the wages of employees for payment as contributions —

        (i) to —

        (I) an employee benefit plan that is subject to title I of the Employee Retirement Income Security Act of 1974 or under an employee benefit plan which is a governmental plan under section 414(d) of the

Internal Revenue Code of 1986;

(II) a deferred compensation plan under section 457 of the Internal Revenue Code of 1986; or

(III) a tax-deferred annuity under section 403(b) of the Internal Revenue Code of 1986; except that such amount under this subparagraph shall not constitute disposable income as defined in section 1325(b)(2); or

(ii) to a health insurance plan regulated by State law whether or not subject to such title; or

(B) received by an employer from employees for payment as contributions —

(i) to —

(I) an employee benefit plan that is subject to title I of the Employee Retirement Income Security Act of 1974 or under an employee benefit plan which is a governmental plan under section 414(d) of the Internal Revenue Code of 1986;

(II) a deferred compensation plan under section 457 of the Internal Revenue Code of 1986; or

(III) a tax-deferred annuity under section 403(b) of the Internal Revenue Code of 1986; except that such amount under this subparagraph shall not constitute disposable income, as defined in section 1325(b)(2); or

(ii) to a health insurance plan regulated by State law whether or not subject to such title;

(8) subject to subchapter III of chapter 5, any interest of the debtor in property where the debtor pledged or sold tangible personal property (other than securities or written or printed evidences of indebtedness or title) as collateral for a loan or advance of money given by a person licensed under law to make such loans or advances, where —

(A) the tangible personal property is in the possession of the pledgee or transferee;

(B) the debtor has no obligation to repay the money, redeem the collateral, or buy back the property at a stipulated price; and

(C) neither the debtor nor the trustee have exercised any right to redeem provided under the contract or State law, in a timely manner as provided under State law and section 108(b); or

(9) any interest in cash or cash equivalents that constitute proceeds of a sale by the debtor of a money order that is made—

(A) on or after the date that is 14 days prior to the date on which the petition is filed; and

(B) under an agreement with a money order issuer that

prohibits the commingling of such proceeds with property of the debtor (notwithstanding that, contrary to the agreement, the proceeds may have been commingled with property of the debtor),

unless the money order issuer had not taken action, prior to the filing of the petition, to require compliance with the prohibition.

Paragraph (4) shall not be construed to exclude from the estate any consideration the debtor retains, receives, or is entitled to receive for transferring an interest in liquid or gaseous hydrocarbons pursuant to a farm out agreement.

(c)

(1) Except as provided in paragraph (2) of this subsection, an interest of the debtor in property becomes property of the estate under subsection (a)(1), (a)(2), or (a)(5) of this section notwithstanding any provision in an agreement, transfer instrument, or applicable nonbankruptcy law—

(A) that restricts or conditions transfer of such interest by the debtor; or

(B) that is conditioned on the insolvency or financial condition of the debtor, on the commencement of a case under this title, or on the appointment of or taking possession by a trustee in a case under this title or a custodian before such commencement, and that effects or gives an option to effect a forfeiture, modification, or termination of the debtor's interest in property.

(2) A restriction on the transfer of a beneficial interest of the debtor in a trust that is enforceable under applicable nonbankruptcy law is enforceable in a case under this title.

(d) Property in which the debtor holds, as of the commencement of the case, only legal title and not an equitable interest, such as a mortgage secured by real property, or an interest in such a mortgage, sold by the debtor but as to which the debtor retains legal title to service or supervise the servicing of such mortgage or interest, becomes property of the estate under subsection (a)(1) or (2) of this section only to the extent of the debtor's legal title to such property, but not to the extent of any equitable interest in such property that the debtor does not hold.

(e) In determining whether any of the relationships specified in paragraph (5)(A) or (6)(A) of subsection (b) exists, a legally adopted child of an individual (and a child who is a member of an individual's household, if placed with such individual by an authorized placement agency for legal adoption by such individual), or a foster child of an individual (if such child has as the child's principal place of abode the home of the debtor and is a member of the debtor's household) shall be treated as a child of such individual by blood.

(f) Notwithstanding any other provision of this title, property that is held by a debtor that is a corporation described in section 501(c)(3) of the Internal Revenue Code of 1986 and exempt from tax under section 501(a) of such

Code may be transferred to an entity that is not such a corporation, but only under the same conditions as would apply if the debtor had not filed a case under this title.

§ 544   Trustee as Lien Creditor and as Successor to Certain Creditors and Purchasers.

(a) The trustee shall have, as of the commencement of the case, and without regard to any knowledge of the trustee or of any creditor, the rights and powers of, or may avoid any transfer of property of the debtor or any obligation incurred by the debtor that is voidable by —

> (1) a creditor that extends credit to the debtor at the time of the commencement of the case, and that obtains, at such time and with respect to such credit, a judicial lien on all property on which a creditor on a simple contract could have obtained such a judicial lien, whether or not such a creditor exists;
>
> (2) a creditor that extends credit to the debtor at the time of the commencement of the case, and obtains, at such time and with respect to such credit, an execution against the debtor that is returned unsatisfied at such time, whether or not such a creditor exists; or
>
> (3) a bona fide purchaser of real property, other than fixtures, from the debtor, against whom applicable law permits such transfer to be perfected, that obtains the status of a bona fide purchaser and has perfected such transfer at the time of the commencement of the case, whether or not such a purchaser exists.

(b)   (1) Except as provided in paragraph (2), the trustee may avoid any transfer of an interest of the debtor in property or any obligation incurred by the debtor that is voidable under applicable law by a creditor holding an unsecured claim that is allowable under section 502 of this title or that is not allowable only under section 502(e) of this title.

(2) Paragraph (1) shall not apply to a transfer of a charitable contribution (as that term is defined in section 548(d)(3)) that is not covered under section 548(a)(1)(B), by reason of section 548(a)(2). Any claim by any person to recover a transferred contribution described in the preceding sentence under Federal or State law in a Federal or State court shall be preempted by the commencement of the case.

§ 547   Preferences

(a) In this section—

> (1) "inventory" means personal property leased or furnished, held for sale or lease, or to be furnished under a contract for service, raw materials, work in process, or materials used or consumed in a business, including farm products such as crops or livestock, held for sale or lease;
>
> (2) "new value" means money or money's worth in goods, services,

or new credit, or release by a transferee of property previously transferred to such transferee in a transaction that is neither void nor voidable by the debtor or the trustee under any applicable law, including proceeds of such property, but does not include an obligation substituted for an existing obligation;

(3) "receivable" means right to payment, whether or not such right has been earned by performance; and

(4) a debt for a tax is incurred on the day when such tax is last payable without penalty, including any extension.

(b) Except as provided in subsections (c) and (i) of this section, the trustee may avoid any transfer of an interest of the debtor in property—

(1) to or for the benefit of a creditor;

(2) for or on account of an antecedent debt owed by the debtor before such transfer was made;

(3) made while the debtor was insolvent;

(4) made—

    (A) on or within 90 days before the date of the filing of the petition; or

    (B) between ninety days and one year before the date of the filing of the petition, if such creditor at the time of such transfer was an insider; and

(5) that enables such creditor to receive more than such creditor would receive if—

    (A) the case were a case under chapter 7 of this title;

    (B) the transfer had not been made; and

    (C) such creditor received payment of such debt to the extent provided by the provisions of this title.

(c) The trustee may not avoid under this section a transfer—

(1) to the extent that such transfer was—

    (A) intended by the debtor and the creditor to or for whose benefit such transfer was made to be a contemporaneous exchange for new value given to the debtor; and

    (B) in fact a substantially contemporaneous exchange;

(2) to the extent that such transfer was in payment of a debt incurred by the debtor in the ordinary course of business or financial affairs of the debtor and the transferee and such transfer was

    (A) made in the ordinary course of business or financial affairs of the debtor and the transferee; or

    (B) made according to ordinary business terms;

(3) that creates a security interest in property acquired by the debtor—

    (A) to the extent such security interest secures new value that was—

        (i) given at or after the signing of a security agreement that contains a description of such property as collateral;

        (ii) given by or on behalf of the secured party under

such agreement;

(iii) given to enable the debtor to acquire such property; and

(iv) in fact used by the debtor to acquire such property; and

(B) that is perfected on or before 30 days after the debtor receives possession of such property;

(4) to or for the benefit of a creditor, to the extent that, after such transfer, such creditor gave new value to or for the benefit of the debtor—

(A) not secured by an otherwise unavoidable security interest; and

(B) on account of which new value the debtor did not make an otherwise unavoidable transfer to or for the benefit of such creditor;

(5) that creates a perfected security interest in inventory or a receivable or the proceeds of either, except to the extent that the aggregate of all such transfers to the transferee caused a reduction, as of the date of the filing of the petition and to the prejudice of other creditors holding unsecured claims, of any amount by which the debt secured by such security interest exceeded the value of all security interests for such debt on the later of—

(A)

(i) with respect to a transfer to which subsection (b)(4)(A) of this section applies, 90 days before the date of the filing of the petition; or

(ii) with respect to a transfer to which subsection (b)(4)(B) of this section applies, one year before the date of the filing of the petition; or

(B) the date on which new value was first given under the security agreement creating such security interest;

(6) that is the fixing of a statutory lien that is not avoidable under section 545 of this title;

(7) to the extent such transfer was a bona fide payment for a domestic spouse obligation;

(8) if, in a case filed by an individual debtor whose debts are primarily consumer debts, the aggregate value of all property that constitutes or is affected by such transfer is less than $600; or

(9) if, in a case filed by a debtor whose debts are not primarily consumer debts, the aggregate value of all property that constitutes or is affected by such transfer is less than $5,000.

(d) The trustee may avoid a transfer of an interest in property of the debtor transferred to or for the benefit of a surety to secure reimbursement of such a surety that furnished a bond or other obligation to dissolve a judicial lien that would have been avoidable by the trustee under subsection (b) of this section. The liability of such surety under such bond or obligation shall be discharged to the extent of the value of such property recovered by the trustee or the amount paid to the trustee.

(e)

  (1) For the purposes of this section—

    (A) a transfer of real property other than fixtures, but including the interest of a seller or purchaser under a contract for the sale of real property, is perfected when a bona fide purchaser of such property from the debtor against whom applicable law permits such transfer to be perfected cannot acquire an interest that is superior to the interest of the transferee; and

    (B) a transfer of a fixture or property other than real property is perfected when a creditor on a simple contract cannot acquire a judicial lien that is superior to the interest of the transferee.

  (2) For the purposes of this section, except as provided in paragraph (3) of this subsection, a transfer is made—

    (A) at the time such transfer takes effect between the transferor and the transferee, if such transfer is perfected at, or within 30 days after, such time, except as provided in subsection (c)(3)(B);

    (B) at the time such transfer is perfected, if such transfer is perfected after such 30 days; or

    (C) immediately before the date of the filing of the petition, if such transfer is not perfected at the later of—

      (i) the commencement of the case; or

      (ii) 30 days after such transfer takes effect between the transferor and the transferee.

  (3) For the purposes of this section, a transfer is not made until the debtor has acquired rights in the property transferred.

(f) For the purposes of this section, the debtor is presumed to have been insolvent on and during the 90 days immediately preceding the date of the filing of the petition.

(g) For the purposes of this section, the trustee has the burden of proving the avoidability of a transfer under subsection (b) of this section, and the creditor or party in interest against whom recovery or avoidance is sought has the burden of proving the nonavoidability of a transfer under subsection (c) of this section.

(h) The trustee may not avoid a transfer if such transfer was made as a part of an alternative repayment schedule between the debtor and any creditor of the debtor created by an approved nonprofit budgeting and credit counseling agency.

(i) If the trustee avoids under subsection (b) a transfer made between 90 days and 1 year before the date of the filing of the petition, by the debtor to an entity that is not an insider for the benefit of a creditor that is an insider, such transfer shall be considered to be avoided under this section only with respect to the creditor that is an insider.

§ 548　Fraudulent transfers and obligations

(a)

(1) The trustee may avoid any transfer (including any transfer to or for the benefit of an insider under an employment contract)of an interest of the debtor in property, or any obligation (including any obligation to or for the benefit of an insider under an employment contract) incurred by the debtor, that was made or incurred on or within one year before the date of the filing of the petition, if the debtor voluntarily or involuntarily—

    (A) made such transfer or incurred such obligation with actual intent to hinder, delay, or defraud any entity to which the debtor was or became, on or after the date that such transfer was made or such obligation was incurred, indebted; or

    (B)

        (i) received less than a reasonably equivalent value in exchange for such transfer or obligation; and

        (ii)

        (I) was insolvent on the date that such transfer was made or such obligation was incurred, or became insolvent as a result of such transfer or obligation;

        (II) was engaged in business or a transaction, or was about to engage in business or a transaction, for which any property remaining with the debtor was an unreasonably small capital; or

        (III) intended to incur, or believed that the debtor would incur, debts that would be beyond the debtor's ability to pay as such debts matured; or

        (IV) made under such transfer to or for the benefit of an insider, under an employment contract and not in the ordinary course of business.

(2) A transfer of a charitable contribution to a qualified religious or charitable entity or organization shall not be considered to be a transfer covered under paragraph (1)(B) in any case in which—

    (A) the amount of that contribution does not exceed 15 percent of the gross annual income of the debtor for the year in which the transfer of the contribution is made; or

    (B) the contribution made by a debtor exceeded the percentage amount of gross annual income specified in subparagraph (A), if the transfer was consistent with the practices of the debtor in making charitable contributions.

(b) The trustee of a partnership debtor may avoid any transfer of an interest of the debtor in property, or any obligation incurred by the debtor, that was made or incurred on or within 2 years before the date of the filing of the petition, to a general partner in the debtor, if the debtor was insolvent on the date such transfer was made or such obligation was incurred, or became insolvent as a result of such transfer or obligation.

(c) Except to the extent that a transfer or obligation voidable under this section is voidable under section 544, 545, or 547 of this title, a transferee or obligee of such a transfer or obligation that takes for value and in good faith has a lien on or may retain any interest transferred or may enforce any obligation incurred, as the case may be, to the extent that such transferee or obligee gave value to the debtor in exchange for such transfer or obligation.

(d)

> **(1)** For the purposes of this section, a transfer is made when such transfer is so perfected that a bona fide purchaser from the debtor against whom applicable law permits such transfer to be perfected cannot acquire an interest in the property transferred that is superior to the interest in such property of the transferee, but if such transfer is not so perfected before the commencement of the case, such transfer is made immediately before the date of the filing of the petition.
>
> **(2)** In this section—
>
>> **(A)** "value" means property, or satisfaction or securing of a present or antecedent debt of the debtor, but does not include an unperformed promise to furnish support to the debtor or to a relative of the debtor;
>>
>> **(B)** a commodity broker, forward contract merchant, stockbroker, financial institution, financial participant or securities clearing agency that receives a margin payment, as defined in section 101, 741, or 761 of this title, or settlement payment, as defined in section 101 or 741 of this title, takes for value to the extent of such payment;
>>
>> **(C)** a repo participant or financial participant that receives a margin payment, as defined in section 741 or 761 of this title, or settlement payment, as defined in section 741 of this title, in connection with a repurchase agreement, takes for value to the extent of such payment; and
>>
>> **(D)** a swap participant or financial participant that receives a transfer in connection with a swap agreement takes for value to the extent of such transfer; and
>>
>> **(E)** a master netting agreement participant that receives a transfer in connection with a master netting agreement or any individual contract covered thereby takes for value to the extent of such transfer, except that, with respect to a transfer under any individual contract covered thereby, to the extent that such master netting agreement participant otherwise did not take (or is otherwise not deemed to have taken) such transfer for value.
>
> **(3)** In this section, the term "charitable contribution" means a charitable contribution, as that term is defined in section 170(c) of the Internal Revenue Code of 1986, if that contribution—
>
>> **(A)** is made by a natural person; and
>>
>> **(B)** consists of—
>>
>>> **(i)** a financial instrument (as that term is defined in section 731(c)(2)(C) of the Internal Revenue Code

of 1986); or

(ii) cash.

(4) In this section, the term "qualified religious or charitable entity or organization" means—

(A) an entity described in section 170(c)(1) of the Internal Revenue Code of 1986; or

(B) an entity or organization described in section 170(c)(2) of the Internal Revenue Code of 1986.

(e) **(1)** In addition to any transfer that the trustee may otherwise avoid, the trustee may avoid any transfer of an interest of the debtor in property that was made on or within 10 years before the date of the filing of the petition, if —

(A) such transfer was made to a self-settled trust or similar device;

(B) such transfer was by the debtor;

(C) the debtor is a beneficiary of such trust or similar device; and

(D) the debtor made such transfer with actual intent to hinder, delay, or defraud any entity to which the debtor was or became, on or after the date that such transfer was made, indebted.

(2) For the purposes of this subsection, a transfer includes a transfer made in anticipation of any money judgment, settlement, civil penalty, equitable order, or criminal fine incurred by, or which the debtor believed would be incurred by —

(A) any violation of the securities laws (as defined in section 3(a)(47) of the Securities Exchange Act of 1934 (15 U.S.C. 78c(a)(47))), any State securities laws, or any regulation or order issued under Federal securities laws or State securities laws; or

(B) fraud, deceit, or manipulation in a fiduciary capacity or in connection with the purchase or sale of any security registered under section 12 or 15(d) of the Securities Exchange Act of 1934 (15 U.S.C. 78l and 78o(d)) or under section 6 of the Securities Act of 1933 (15 U.S.C. 77f).

§ 550 Liability of Transferee of Avoided Transfer.

(a) Except as otherwise provided in this section, to the extent that a transfer is avoided under section 544, 545, 547, 548, 549, 553(b), or 724(a) of this title, the trustee may recover, for the benefit of the estate, the property transferred, or, if the court so orders, the value of such property, from —

(1) the initial transferee of such transfer or the entity for whose benefit such transfer was made; or

(2) any immediate or mediate transferee of such initial transferee.

(b) The trustee may not recover under section (a)(2) of this section from —

(1) a transferee that takes for value, including satisfaction or securing of a present or antecedent debt, in good faith, and without knowledge of the voidability of the transfer avoided; or

(2) any immediate or mediate good faith transferee of such transferee.

(c) If a transfer made between 90 days and one year before the filing of the petition —

(1) is avoided under section 547(b) of this title; and

(2) was made for the benefit of a creditor that at the time of such transfer was an insider; the trustee may not recover under subsection (a) from a transferee that is not an insider.

(d) The trustee is entitled to only a single satisfaction under subsection (a) of this section.

(e)(1) A good faith transferee from whom the trustee may recover under subsection (a) of this section has a lien on the property recovered to secure the lesser of —

(A) the cost, to such transferee, of any improvement made after the transfer, less the amount of any profit realized by or accruing to such transferee from such property; and

(B) any increase in the value of such property as a result of such improvement, of the property transferred.

(2) In this subsection, "improvement" includes —

(A) physical additions or changes to the property transferred;

(B) repairs to such property;

(C) payment of any tax on such property;

(D) payment of any debt secured by a lien on such property that is superior or equal to the rights of the trustee; and

(E) preservation of such property.

(f) An action or proceeding under this section may not be commenced after the earlier of —

(1) one year after the avoidance of the transfer on account of which recovery under this section is sought; or

(2) the time the case is closed or dismissed.

§ 551   Automatic Preservation of Avoided Transfer

Any transfer avoided under section 522, 544, 545, 547, 548, 549, or 724(a) of this title, or any lien void under section 506(d) of this title, is preserved for the benefit of the estate but only with respect to property of the estate.

§ 553   Setoff

(a)   Except as otherwise provided in this section and in sections 362 and 363 of this title, this title does not affect any right of a creditor to offset a mutual debt owing by such creditor to the debtor that arose before the commencement of the case under this title against a claim of such creditor against the debtor that arose before the commencement of the case, except to the extent that —

(1) the claim of such creditor against the debtor is disallowed;

(2) such claim was transferred, by an entity other than the debtor, to such creditor —

  (A) after the commencement of the case; or

  (B)   **(i)** after 90 days before the date of the filing of the petition; and

    (ii) while the debtor was insolvent (except for a setoff of a kind described in section 362(b)(6), 362(b)(7), 362(b)(17), 362(b)(27), 555, 556, 559, 560, or 561); or

(3) the debt owed to the debtor by such creditor was incurred by such creditor —

  (A) after 90 days before the date of the filing of the petition;

  (B) while the debtor was insolvent; and

  (C) for the purpose of obtaining a right of setoff against the debtor (except for a setoff of a kind described in section 362(b)(6), 362(b)(7), 362(b)(17), 362(b)(27), 555, 556, 559, 560, or 561).

  (b)   **(1)** Except with respect to a setoff of a kind described in section 362(b)(6), 362(b)(7), 362(b)(17), 362(b)(27), 555, 556, 559, 560, 561, 365(h), 546(h), or 365(i)(2) of this title, if a creditor offsets a mutual debt owing to the debtor against a claim against the debtor on or within 90 days before the date of the filing of the petition, then the trustee may recover from such creditor the amount so offset to the extent that any insufficiency on the date of such setoff is less than the insufficiency on the later of —

(A) 90 days before the date of the filing of the petition; and

(B) the first date during the 90 days immediately preceding the date of the filing of the petition on which there is an insufficiency.

  (2) In this subsection, "insufficiency" means amount, if any, by which a claim against the debtor exceeds a mutual debt owing to the debtor by the holder of such claim.

  (c) For the purposes of this section, the debtor is presumed to have been insolvent on and during the 90 days immediately preceding the date of the filing of the petition.

§ 1102 Creditors' and equity security holders' committees

  (a)

  (1) Except as provided in paragraph (3), as soon as practicable after the order for relief under chapter 11 of this title, the United States trustee shall appoint a committee of creditors holding unsecured claims and may appoint additional committees of creditors or of equity security holders as the United States trustee deems appropriate.

  (2) On request of a party in interest, the court may order the appointment of additional committees of creditors or of equity security holders if necessary to assure adequate representation of creditors or of equity security holders. The United States trustee shall appoint any such committee.

(3) On request of a party in interest in a case in which the debtor is a small business and for cause, the court may order that a committee of creditors not be appointed.

(4) On request of a party in interest and after notice and a hearing, the court may order the **United States** trustee to change the membership of a committee appointed under this subsection, if the court determines that the change is necessary to ensure adequate representation of creditors or equity security holders. The court may order the United States trustee to increase the number of members of a committee to include a creditor that is a small business concern (as described in section 3(a)(1) of the Small Business Act); if the court determines that the creditor holds claims (or the kind represented by the committee) the aggregate amount of which, in comparison to the annual gross revenue of that creditor, is disproportionately large.

(b)

(1) A committee of creditors appointed under subsection (a) of this section shall ordinarily consist of the persons, willing to serve, that hold the seven largest claims against the debtor of the kinds represented on such committee, or of the members of a committee organized by creditors before the commencement of the case under this chapter, if such committee was fairly chosen and is representative of the different kinds of claims to be represented.

(2) A committee of equity security holders appointed under subsection (a)(2) of this section shall ordinarily consist of the persons, willing to serve, that hold the seven largest amounts of equity securities of the debtor of the kinds represented on such committee.

(3) A committee appointed under subsection (a) shall –

    (A) provide access information to creditors who –

        (i) hold claims of the kind represented by that committee; and

        (ii) are not appointed to that committee

    (B) solicit and receive comments from the creditors described in subparagraph (A); and

    (C) be subject to a court order that compels any additional report or disclosure to be made to the creditors described in subparagraph (A).

§ 1103 Powers and duties of committees

(a) At a scheduled meeting of a committee appointed under section 1102 of this title, at which a majority of the members of such committee are present, and with the court's approval, such committee may select and authorize the employment by such committee of one or more attorneys, accountants, or other agents, to represent or perform services for such committee.

(b) An attorney or accountant employed to represent a committee appointed under section 1102 of this title may not, while employed by such committee, represent any other entity having an adverse interest in connection with the case. Representation of one or more creditors of the same class as represented by the committee shall not per se constitute the representation of an adverse interest.

(c) A committee appointed under section 1102 of this title may—

(1) consult with the trustee or debtor in possession concerning the administration of the case;

(2) investigate the acts, conduct, assets, liabilities, and financial condition of the debtor, the operation of the debtor's business and the desirability of the continuance of such business, and any other matter relevant to the case or to the formulation of a plan;

(3) participate in the formulation of a plan, advise those represented by such committee of such committee's determinations as to any plan formulated, and collect and file with the court acceptances or rejections of a plan;

(4) request the appointment of a trustee or examiner under section 1104 of this title; and

(5) perform such other services as are in the interest of those represented.

(d) As soon as practicable after the appointment of a committee under section 1102 of this title, the trustee shall meet with such committee to transact such business as may be necessary and proper.

§ 1106 Duties of trustee and examiner

(a) A trustee shall—

(1) perform the duties of a trustee specified in sections 704 (2), 704 (5), 704 (7), 704 (8), and 704 (9) of this title;

(2) if the debtor has not done so, file the list, schedule, and statement required under section 521 (1) of this title;

(3) except to the extent that the court orders otherwise, investigate the acts, conduct, assets, liabilities, and financial condition of the debtor, the operation of the debtor's business and the desirability of the continuance of such business, and any other matter relevant to the case or to the formulation of a plan;

(4) as soon as practicable—

(i)   (b)file a statement of any investigation conducted under paragraph (3) of this subsection, including any fact ascertained pertaining to fraud, dishonesty, incompetence, misconduct, mismanagement, or irregularity in the management of the affairs of the debtor, or to a cause of action available to the estate; and

(ii) transmit a copy or a summary of any such statement to any creditors' committee or equity security holders' committee, to any indenture trustee, and to such other entity as the court designates;

(5) as soon as practicable, file a plan under section 1121 of this title, file a report of why the trustee will not file a plan, or recommend conversion of the case to a case under chapter 7, 12, or 13 of this title or dismissal of the case;

(6) for any year for which the debtor has not filed a tax return required by law, furnish, without personal liability, such information as may be required by the governmental unit with which such tax return was to be filed, in light of the condition of the debtor's books and records and the availability of such information; and

(7) after confirmation of a plan, file such reports as are necessary or as the court orders.

(b) An examiner appointed under section 1104 (d) of this title shall perform the duties specified in paragraphs (3) and (4) of subsection (a) of this section, and, except to the extent that the court orders otherwise, any other duties of the trustee that the court orders the debtor in possession not to perform. . . .

§ 1107 Rights, powers, and duties of debtor in possession

(a) Subject to any limitations on a trustee serving in a case under this chapter, and to such limitations or conditions as the court prescribes, a debtor in possession shall have all the rights, other than the right to compensation under section 330 of this title, and powers, and shall perform all the functions and duties, except the duties specified in sections 1106 (a)(2), (3), and (4) of this title, of a trustee serving in a case under this chapter.

(b) Notwithstanding section 327 (a) of this title, a person is not disqualified for employment under section 327 of this title by a debtor in possession solely because of such person's employment by or representation of the debtor before the commencement of the case.

§ 1108 Authorization to operate business

Unless the court, on request of a party in interest and after notice and a hearing, orders otherwise, the trustee may operate the debtor's business.

§ 1111 Claims and interests

(a) A proof of claim or interest is deemed filed under section 501 of this title for any claim or interest that appears in the schedules filed under section 521 (1) or 1106 (a)(2) of this title, except a claim or interest that is scheduled as disputed, contingent, or unliquidated.

(b)

(1)

(A) A claim secured by a lien on property of the estate shall be allowed or disallowed under section 502 of this title the same as if the holder of such claim had recourse against the debtor on account of such claim, whether or not such holder has such recourse, unless—

(i) the class of which such claim is a part elects, by at least two-thirds in amount and more than half in number of allowed claims of such class, application of paragraph (2) of this subsection; or

(ii) such holder does not have such recourse and such property is sold under section 363 of this title or is to be sold under the plan.

(B) A class of claims may not elect application of paragraph (2) of this subsection if—

(i) the interest on account of such claims of the holders of such claims in such property is of inconsequential value; or

(ii) the holder of a claim of such class has recourse against the debtor on account of such claim and such property is sold under section 363 of this title or is to be sold under the plan.

(2) If such an election is made, then notwithstanding section 506 (a) of this title, such claim is a secured claim to the extent that such claim is allowed.

§ 1121 Who may file a plan

(a) The debtor may file a plan with a petition commencing a voluntary case, or at any time in a voluntary case or an involuntary case.

(b) Except as otherwise provided in this section, only the debtor may file a plan until after 120 days after the date of the order for relief under this chapter.

(c) Any party in interest, including the debtor, the trustee, a creditors' committee, an equity security holders' committee, a creditor, an equity security holder, or any indenture trustee, may file a plan if and only if—

(1) a trustee has been appointed under this chapter;

(2) the debtor has not filed a plan before 120 days after the date of the order for relief under this chapter; or

(3) the debtor has not filed a plan that has been accepted, before 180 days after the date of the order for relief under this chapter, by each class of claims or interests that is impaired under the plan.

(d)

(1) Subject to paragraph (2), on request of a party in interest made within the respective periods specified in subsections (b) and (c) of this section and after notice and a hearing, the court may for cause reduce or increase the 120-day period or the 180-day period referred to in this section.

(2)

(A) The 120-day period specified in paragraph (1) may not be extended beyond a date that is 18 months after the date of the order for relief under this chapter.

(B) The 180-day period specified in paragraph (1) may not be extended beyond a date that is 20 months after the

date of the order for relief under this chapter.
(e) In a small business case—
- **(1)** only the debtor may file a plan after 180 days after the date of the order for relief, unless that period is –
  - **(A)** extended as provided by this subsection, after notice and a hearing; or
  - **(B)** the court, for cause, orders otherwise;
- **(2)** the plan and a disclosure statement (if any) shall be filed not later than 300 days after the date of the order for relief; and
- **(3)** the time periods specified in paragraphs (1) and (2), and the time fixed in section 1129(e) within which the plan shall be confirmed, may be extended only if –
  - **(A)** the debtor, after providing notice to parties in interest (including the United States trustee), demonstrates by a preponderance of the evidence that it is more likely than not that the court will confirm a plan within a reasonable period of time;
  - **(B)** a new deadline is imposed at the time the extension is grated; and
  - **(C)** the order extending time is signed before the existing deadline has expired.

§ 1122 Classification of claims or interests

(a) Except as provided in subsection (b) of this section, a plan may place a claim or an interest in a particular class only if such claim or interest is substantially similar to the other claims or interests of such class.

(b) A plan may designate a separate class of claims consisting only of every unsecured claim that is less than or reduced to an amount that the court approves as reasonable and necessary for administrative convenience.

§ 1123 Contents of plan

(a) Notwithstanding any otherwise applicable nonbankruptcy law, a plan shall—

- **(1)** designate, subject to section 1122 of this title, classes of claims, other than claims of a kind specified in section 507 (a)(2), 507 (a)(3), or 507 (a)(8) of this title, and classes of interests;
- **(2)** specify any class of claims or interests that is not impaired under the plan;
- **(3)** specify the treatment of any class of claims or interests that is impaired under the plan;
- **(4)** provide the same treatment for each claim or interest of a particular class, unless the holder of a particular claim or interest agrees to a less favorable treatment of such particular claim or interest;
- **(5)** provide adequate means for the plan's implementation, such as—

(A) retention by the debtor of all or any part of the property of the estate;

(B) transfer of all or any part of the property of the estate to one or more entities, whether organized before or after the confirmation of such plan;

(C) merger or consolidation of the debtor with one or more persons;

(D) sale of all or any part of the property of the estate, either subject to or free of any lien, or the distribution of all or any part of the property of the estate among those having an interest in such property of the estate;

(E) satisfaction or modification of any lien;

(F) cancellation or modification of any indenture or similar instrument;

(G) curing or waiving of any default;

(H) extension of a maturity date or a change in an interest rate or other term of outstanding securities;

(I) amendment of the debtor's charter; or

(J) issuance of securities of the debtor, or of any entity referred to in subparagraph (B) or (C) of this paragraph, for cash, for property, for existing securities, or in exchange for claims or interests, or for any other appropriate purpose;

(6) provide for the inclusion in the charter of the debtor, if the debtor is a corporation, or of any corporation referred to in paragraph (5)(B) or (5)(C) of this subsection, of a provision prohibiting the issuance of nonvoting equity securities, and providing, as to the several classes of securities possessing voting power, an appropriate distribution of such power among such classes, including, in the case of any class of equity securities having a preference over another class of equity securities with respect to dividends, adequate provisions for the election of directors representing such preferred class in the event of default in the payment of such dividends; and

(7) contain only provisions that are consistent with the interests of creditors and equity security holders and with public policy with respect to the manner of selection of any officer, director, or trustee under the plan and any successor to such officer, director, or trustee; and

(8) in a case in which the debtor is an individual, provide for the payment to creditors under the plan of all or such portion of earnings from personal services performed by the debtor after the commencement of the case or other future income of the debtor as is necessary for the execution of the plan.

(b) Subject to subsection (a) of this section, a plan may—

(1) impair or leave unimpaired any class of claims, secured or unsecured, or of interests;

(2) subject to section 365 of this title, provide for the assumption,

rejection, or assignment of any executory contract or unexpired lease of the debtor not previously rejected under such section;

(3) provide for—

(A) the settlement or adjustment of any claim or interest belonging to the debtor or to the estate; or

(B) the retention and enforcement by the debtor, by the trustee, or by a representative of the estate appointed for such purpose, of any such claim or interest;

(4) provide for the sale of all or substantially all of the property of the estate, and the distribution of the proceeds of such sale among holders of claims or interests;

(5) modify the rights of holders of secured claims, other than a claim secured only by a security interest in real property that is the debtor's principal residence, or of holders of unsecured claims, or leave unaffected the rights of holders of any class of claims; and

(6) include any other appropriate provision not inconsistent with the applicable provisions of this title.

(c) In a case concerning an individual, a plan proposed by an entity other than the debtor may not provide for the use, sale, or lease of property exempted under section 522 of this title, unless the debtor consents to such use, sale, or lease.

(d) Notwithstanding subsection (a) of this section and sections 506 (b), 1129 (a)(7), and 1129 (b) of this title, if it is proposed in a plan to cure a default the amount necessary to cure the default shall be determined in accordance with the underlying agreement and applicable nonbankruptcy law.

§ 1124 Impairment of claims or interests

Except as provided in section 1123 (a)(4) of this title, a class of claims or interests is impaired under a plan unless, with respect to each claim or interest of such class, the plan—

(1) leaves unaltered the legal, equitable, and contractual rights to which such claim or interest entitles the holder of such claim or interest; or

(2) notwithstanding any contractual provision or applicable law that entitles the holder of such claim or interest to demand or receive accelerated payment of such claim or interest after the occurrence of a default—

(A) cures any such default that occurred before or after the commencement of the case under this title, other than a default of a kind specified in section 365 (b)(2) of this title or of a kind that section 365(b)(2) expressly does not require to be cured;

(B) reinstates the maturity of such claim or interest as such maturity existed before such default;

(C) compensates the holder of such claim or interest for any damages incurred as a result of any reasonable reliance by such holder on such contractual provision or such applicable law; and

(D) if such claim or such interest arises from any failure to perform a nonmonetary obligation, other than a default arising from failure to operate a nonresidential real property lease subject to section 365(b)(1)(A), compensates the holder of such claim or such interest (other than the debtor or an insider) for any actual pecuniary loss incurred by such holder as a result of such failure; and

(E) does not otherwise alter the legal, equitable, or contractual rights to which such claim or interest entitles the holder of such claim or interest.

§ 1125 Postpetition disclosure and solicitation

(a) In this section—

(1) "adequate information" means information of a kind, and in sufficient detail, as far as is reasonably practicable in light of the nature and history of the debtor and the condition of the debtor's books and records, including a discussion of the potential material Federal tax consequences of the plan to the debtor, and a hypothetical investor typical of the holders of claims or interests in the case that would enable such a hypothetical investor of the relevant class to make an informed judgment about the plan, but adequate information need not include such information about any other possible or proposed plan and in determining whether a disclosure statement provides adequate information, the court shall consider the complexity of the case, the benefit of additional information to creditors another parties in interest, and the cost of providing additional information; and

(2) "investor typical of holders of claims or interests of the relevant class" means investor having—

(A) a claim or interest of the relevant class;

(B) such a relationship with the debtor as the holders of other claims or interests of such class generally have; and

(C) such ability to obtain such information from sources other than the disclosure required by this section as holders of claims or interests in such class generally have.

(b) An acceptance or rejection of a plan may not be solicited after the commencement of the case under this title from a holder of a claim or interest with respect to such claim or interest, unless, at the time of or before such solicitation, there is transmitted to such holder the plan or a summary of the plan, and a written disclosure statement approved, after notice and a hearing, by the court as containing adequate information. The court may approve a disclosure statement without a valuation of the debtor or an appraisal of the debtor's assets.

(c) The same disclosure statement shall be transmitted to each holder of a claim or interest of a particular class, but there may be transmitted different disclosure statements, differing in amount, detail, or kind of information, as between classes.

(d) Whether a disclosure statement required under subsection (b) of this section contains adequate information is not governed by any otherwise applicable nonbankruptcy law, rule, or regulation, but an agency or official whose duty is to administer or enforce such a law, rule, or regulation may be heard on the issue of whether a disclosure statement contains adequate information. Such an agency or official may not appeal from, or otherwise seek review of, an order approving a disclosure statement.

(e) A person that solicits acceptance or rejection of a plan, in good faith and in compliance with the applicable provisions of this title, or that participates, in good faith and in compliance with the applicable provisions of this title, in the offer, issuance, sale, or purchase of a security, offered or sold under the plan, of the debtor, of an affiliate participating in a joint plan with the debtor, or of a newly organized successor to the debtor under the plan, is not liable, on account of such solicitation or participation, for violation of any applicable law, rule, or regulation governing solicitation of acceptance or rejection of a plan or the offer, issuance, sale, or purchase of securities.

(f) Notwithstanding subsection (b), in a small business case—

(1) the court may determine that the plan itself provides adequate information and that a separate disclosure statement in not necessary;

(2) the court may approve a disclosure statement submitted on standard forms approved by the court or adopted under section 2075 of title 28; and

(3)

(A) the court may conditionally approve a disclosure statement subject to final approval after notice and a hearing;

(B) acceptances and rejections of a plan may be solicited based on a conditionally approved disclosure statement if the debtor provides adequate information to each holder of a claim or interest that is solicited, but a conditionally approved disclosure statement shall be mailed not later than 25 days before the date of the hearing on confirmation of the plan; and

(C) the hearing on the disclosure statement may be combined with the hearing on confirmation of a plan.

(g) Notwithstanding subsection (b), an acceptance or rejection of the plan may be solicited from a holder of a claim or interest if such solicitation complies with applicable nonbankrupcy law and if such holder was solicited before the commencement of the case in a manner complying with applicable nonbankruptcy law.

§ 1126 Acceptance of plan

(a) The holder of a claim or interest allowed under section 502 of this title may accept or reject a plan. If the United States is a creditor or equity security holder, the Secretary of the Treasury may accept or reject the plan on behalf of the United States.

(b) For the purposes of subsections (c) and (d) of this section, a holder of a claim or interest that has accepted or rejected the plan before the commencement of the case under this title is deemed to have accepted or rejected such plan, as the case may be, if—

(1) the solicitation of such acceptance or rejection was in compliance with any applicable nonbankruptcy law, rule, or regulation governing the adequacy of disclosure in connection with such solicitation; or

(2) if there is not any such law, rule, or regulation, such acceptance or rejection was solicited after disclosure to such holder of adequate information, as defined in section 1125 (a) of this title.

(c) A class of claims has accepted a plan if such plan has been accepted by creditors, other than any entity designated under subsection (e) of this section, that hold at least two-thirds in amount and more than one-half in number of the allowed claims of such class held by creditors, other than any entity designated under subsection (e) of this section, that have accepted or rejected such plan.

(d) A class of interests has accepted a plan if such plan has been accepted by holders of such interests, other than any entity designated under subsection (e) of this section, that hold at least two-thirds in amount of the allowed interests of such class held by holders of such interests, other than any entity designated under subsection (e) of this section, that have accepted or rejected such plan.

(e) On request of a party in interest, and after notice and a hearing, the court may designate any entity whose acceptance or rejection of such plan was not in good faith, or was not solicited or procured in good faith or in accordance with the provisions of this title.

(f) Notwithstanding any other provision of this section, a class that is not impaired under a plan, and each holder of a claim or interest of such class, are conclusively presumed to have accepted the plan, and solicitation of acceptances with respect to such class from the holders of claims or interests of such class is not required.

(g) Notwithstanding any other provision of this section, a class is deemed not to have accepted a plan if such plan provides that the claims or interests of such class do not entitle the holders of such claims or interests to receive or retain any property under the plan on account of such claims or interests.

§ 1128 Confirmation hearing

(a) After notice, the court shall hold a hearing on confirmation of a plan.

(b) A party in interest may object to confirmation of a plan.

§ 1129 Confirmation of plan

(a) The court shall confirm a plan only if all of the following requirements are met:

(1) The plan complies with the applicable provisions of this title.

(2) The proponent of the plan complies with the applicable provisions of this title.

(3) The plan has been proposed in good faith and not by any means forbidden by law.

(4) Any payment made or to be made by the proponent, by the debtor, or by a person issuing securities or acquiring property under the plan, for services or for costs and expenses in or in connection with the case, or in connection with the plan and incident to the case, has been approved by, or is subject to the approval of, the court as reasonable.

(5)

    (A)

        (i) The proponent of the plan has disclosed the identity and affiliations of any individual proposed to serve, after confirmation of the plan, as a director, officer, or voting trustee of the debtor, an affiliate of the debtor participating in a joint plan with the debtor, or a successor to the debtor under the plan; and

        (ii) the appointment to, or continuance in, such office of such individual, is consistent with the interests of creditors and equity security holders and with public policy; and

    (B) the proponent of the plan has disclosed the identity of any insider that will be employed or retained by the reorganized debtor, and the nature of any compensation for such insider.

(6) Any governmental regulatory commission with jurisdiction, after confirmation of the plan, over the rates of the debtor has approved any rate change provided for in the plan, or such rate change is expressly conditioned on such approval.

(7) With respect to each impaired class of claims or interests—

    (A) each holder of a claim or interest of such class—

        (i) has accepted the plan; or

        (ii) will receive or retain under the plan on account of such claim or interest property of a value, as of the effective date of the plan, that is not less than the amount that such holder would so receive or retain if the debtor were liquidated under chapter 7 of this title on such date; or

    (B) if section 1111 (b)(2) of this title applies to the claims of such class, each holder of a claim of such class will receive or retain under the plan on account of such claim property of a value, as of the effective date of the plan, that is not less than the value of such holder's interest in the estate's interest in the property that secures such claims.

(8) With respect to each class of claims or interests—

    (A) such class has accepted the plan; or

    (B) such class is not impaired under the plan.

(9) Except to the extent that the holder of a particular claim has agreed to a different treatment of such claim, the plan provides that—

(A) with respect to a claim of a kind specified in section 507 (a)(1) or 507 (a)(2) of this title, on the effective date of the plan, the holder of such claim will receive on account of such claim cash equal to the allowed amount of such claim;

(B) with respect to a class of claims of a kind specified in section 507 (a)(3), 507 (a)(4), 507 (a)(5), 507 (a)(6), or 507 (a)(7) of this title, each holder of a claim of such class will receive—

(i) if such class has accepted the plan, deferred cash payments of a value, as of the effective date of the plan, equal to the allowed amount of such claim; or

(ii) if such class has not accepted the plan, cash on the effective date of the plan equal to the allowed amount of such claim; and

(C) with respect to a claim of a kind specified in section 507 (a)(8) of this title, the holder of such claim will receive on account of such claim regular installment payments in cash--

(i) of a total value, as of the effective date of the plan, equal to the allowed amount of such claim;

(ii) over a period ending not later than 5 years after the date of the order for relief under section 301, 302 or 303; and

(iii) in a manner not less favorable than the most favored nonpriority unsecured claim provided for by the plan (other than cash payments made to a class of creditors under section 1122(b)); and

(D) with respect to a secured claim which would otherwise meet the description of an unsecured claim of a governmental unit under 507(a)(8), but for the secured status of that claim, the holder of that claim will receive an account of that claim, cash payments, in the same manner and over the same period, as prescribed in subparagraph (C)

(10) If a class of claims is impaired under the plan, at least one class of claims that is impaired under the plan has accepted the plan, determined without including any acceptance of the plan by any insider.

(11) Confirmation of the plan is not likely to be followed by the liquidation, or the need for further financial reorganization, of the debtor or any successor to the debtor under the plan, unless such liquidation or reorganization is proposed in the plan.

(12) All fees payable under section 1930 of title 28, as determined by the court at the hearing on confirmation of the plan, have been paid or the plan provides for the payment of all such fees on the effective date of the plan.

(13) The plan provides for the continuation after its effective date of payment of all retiree benefits, as that term is defined in section 1114 of this title, at the level established pursuant to subsection (e)(1)(B) or (g) of section 1114 of this title, at any time prior to confirmation of the plan, for the duration of the period the debtor has obligated itself to provide such benefits.

(14) If the debtor is required by a judicial or administrative order, or by statute, to pay a domestic support obligation, the debtor has paid all amounts payable under such order or such statute for such obligation that first became payable after the date of the filing of the petition.

(15) In a case in which the debtor in an individual and in which the holder of an allowed unsecured claim objects to the confirmation of the plan –

> **(A)** the value, as of the effective date of the plan, of the property to be distributed under the plan on account of such claim is not less than the amount of such claim; or
>
> **(B)** the value of the property to be distributed under the plan is not less than the projected disposable income of the debtor (as defined in section 1325(b)(2)) to be received during the 5-year period beginning on the date that the first payment is due under the plan, or during the period for which the plan provides payments, whichever is longer.

(16) All transfers of property of the plan shall be made in accordance with any applicable provisions of nonbankruptcy law that govern the transfer of property by a corporation or trust that is not moneyed, business, or commercial corporation or trust.

(b)

(1) Notwithstanding section 510 (a) of this title, if all of the applicable requirements of subsection (a) of this section other than paragraph (8) are met with respect to a plan, the court, on request of the proponent of the plan, shall confirm the plan notwithstanding the requirements of such paragraph if the plan does not discriminate unfairly, and is fair and equitable, with respect to each class of claims or interests that is impaired under, and has not accepted, the plan.

(2) For the purpose of this subsection, the condition that a plan be fair and equitable with respect to a class includes the following requirements:

> **(A)** With respect to a class of secured claims, the plan provides—
>
> > **(i)**
> >
> > > **(I)** that the holders of such claims retain the liens securing such claims, whether the

property subject to such liens is retained by the debtor or transferred to another entity, to the extent of the allowed amount of such claims; and

(II) that each holder of a claim of such class receive on account of such claim deferred cash payments totaling at least the allowed amount of such claim, of a value, as of the effective date of the plan, of at least the value of such holder's interest in the estate's interest in such property;

(ii) for the sale, subject to section 363 (k) of this title, of any property that is subject to the liens securing such claims, free and clear of such liens, with such liens to attach to the proceeds of such sale, and the treatment of such liens on proceeds under clause (i) or (iii) of this subparagraph; or

(iii) for the realization by such holders of the indubitable equivalent of such claims.

(B) With respect to a class of unsecured claims—

(i) the plan provides that each holder of a claim of such class receive or retain on account of such claim property of a value, as of the effective date of the plan, equal to the allowed amount of such claim; or

(ii) the holder of any claim or interest that is junior to the claims of such class will not receive or retain under the plan on account of such junior claim or interest any property, except that in the case in which the debtor is an individual, the debtor may retain property included in the estate under section 1115, subject to the requirements of subsection (a)(14) of this section.

(C) With respect to a class of interests—

(i) the plan provides that each holder of an interest of such class receive or retain on account of such interest property of a value, as of the effective date of the plan, equal to the greatest of the allowed amount of any fixed liquidation preference to which such holder is entitled, any fixed redemption price to which such holder is entitled, or the value of such interest; or

(ii) the holder of any interest that is junior to the interests of such class will not receive or retain under the plan on account of such junior interest any property.

(c) Notwithstanding subsections (a) and (b) of this section and except as provided in section 1127 (b) of this title, the court may confirm only one plan, unless the order of confirmation in the case has been revoked under section 1144 of this title. If the requirements of subsections (a) and (b) of this section are met with respect to more than one plan, the court shall consider the preferences of creditors and equity security holders in determining which plan to confirm.

(d) Notwithstanding any other provision of this section, on request of a party in interest that is a governmental unit, the court may not confirm a plan if the principal purpose of the plan is the avoidance of taxes or the avoidance of the application of section 5 of the Securities Act of 1933. In any hearing under this subsection, the governmental unit has the burden of proof on the issue of avoidance.

(e) In a small business case, the court shall confirm a plan that complies with the applicable provisions of this title and that is filed in accordance with section 1121(e) not later than 45 days after the plan is filed unless the time for confirmation is extended in accordance with section 1121(e)(3).

§ 1141   Effect of confirmation

(a) Except as provided in subsections (d)(2) and (d)(3) of this section, the provisions of a confirmed plan bind the debtor, any entity issuing securities under the plan, any entity acquiring property under the plan, and any creditor, equity security holder, or general partner in the debtor, whether or not the claim or interest of such creditor, equity security holder, or general partner is impaired under the plan and whether or not such creditor, equity security holder, or general partner has accepted the plan.

(b) Except as otherwise provided in the plan or the order confirming the plan, the confirmation of a plan vests all of the property of the estate in the debtor.

(c) Except as provided in subsections (d)(2) and (d)(3) of this section and except as otherwise provided in the plan or in the order confirming the plan, after confirmation of a plan, the property dealt with by the plan is free and clear of all claims and interests of creditors, equity security holders, and of general partners in the debtor.

(d)

(1) Except as otherwise provided in this subsection, in the plan, or in the order confirming the plan, the confirmation of a plan—

(A) discharges the debtor from any debt that arose before the date of such confirmation, and any debt of a kind specified in section 502 (g), 502 (h), or 502 (i) of this title, whether or not—

(i) a proof of the claim based on such debt is filed or deemed filed under section 501 of this title;

(ii) such claim is allowed under section 502 of this title; or

(iii) the holder of such claim has accepted the plan; and

(B) terminates all rights and interests of equity security

holders and general partners provided for by the plan.

(2) A discharge under this chapter does not discharge a debtor who is an individual from any debt excepted from discharge under section 523 of this title.

(3) The confirmation of a plan does not discharge a debtor if—

(A) the plan provides for the liquidation of all or substantially all of the property of the estate;

(B) the debtor does not engage in business after consummation of the plan; and

(C) the debtor would be denied a discharge under section 727 (a) of this title if the case were a case under chapter 7 of this title.

(4) The court may approve a written waiver of discharge executed by the debtor after the order for relief under this chapter.

(5) In a case in which the debtor is an individual —

(A) unless after notice and a hearing the court orders otherwise for cause, confirmation of the plan does not discharge any debt provided for in the plan until the court grants a discharge on completion of all payments under the plan;

(B) at any time after the confirmation of the plan, and after notice and a hearing, the court may grant a discharge to the debtor who has not completed payments under the plan if —

(i) the value, as of the effective date of the plan, of property actually distributed under the plan on account of each allowed unsecured claim is not less than the amount that would have been paid on such claim if the estate of the debtor had been liquidated under chapter 7 on such date; and

(ii) modification of the plan under section 1127 is not practicable; and

(C) unless after notice and a hearing held not more than 10 days before the date of the entry of the order granting the discharge, the court finds that there is no reasonable cause to believe that —

(i) section 522(q)(1) may be applicable to the debtor; and

(ii) there is pending any proceeding in which the debtor may be found guilty of a felony of the kind described in section 522(q)(1)(A) or liable for a debt of the kind described in section 522(q)(1)(B).

(6) Notwithstanding paragraph (1), the confirmation of a plan does not discharge a debtor that is a corporation from any debt —

(A) of a kind specified in paragraph (2)(A) or (2)(B) of section 523(a) that is owed to a domestic governmental unit, or owed to a person as the result of an action filed under subchapter III of chapter 37 of title 31 or any similar

State statute; or

(B) for a tax or customs duty with respect to which the debtor —

    (i) made a fraudulent return; or

    (ii) willfully attempted in any manner to evade or to defeat such tax or such customs duty.

§ 1142 Implementation of plan

(a) Notwithstanding any otherwise applicable nonbankruptcy law, rule, or regulation relating to financial condition, the debtor and any entity organized or to be organized for the purpose of carrying out the plan shall carry out the plan and shall comply with any orders of the court.

(b) The court may direct the debtor and any other necessary party to execute or deliver or to join in the execution or delivery of any instrument required to effect a transfer of property dealt with by a confirmed plan, and to perform any other act, including the satisfaction of any lien, that is necessary for the consummation of the plan.

§ 1143 Distribution

If a plan requires presentment or surrender of a security or the performance of any other act as a condition to participation in distribution under the plan, such action shall be taken not later than five years after the date of the entry of the order of confirmation. Any entity that has not within such time presented or surrendered such entity's security or taken any such other action that the plan requires may not participate in distribution under the plan.

9 781598 004137